AMERICAN FOOTBALL

HOW THE GAME EVOLVED

By

James E. Herget

2013

TABLE OF CONTENTS

Preface		v
Chapter I	Early Beginnings 1840s – 1869	1
Chapter 2	The Association Game 1869-1874	7
Chapter 3	The Transition to Rugby 1874-1876	15
Chapter 4	The Rugby Game 1876-1880	25
Chapter 5	Moving Away from Rugby 1880-1883	35
Chapter 6	Down the Wrong Path 1884-1894	51
Chapter 7	Criticism and Reaction 1894-1896	69
Chapter 8	The Calm before the Storm 1896-1905	77
Chapter 9	Abolish or Reform? 1905-1910	85
Chapter 10	Completing the Revolution 1910-1912	103
Chapter 11	Realizing the Potential of the New Game 1912-1918	109
Chapter 12	Moving to the Modern Game – Rules 1918-present	115
Chapter 13	Moving to the Modern Game – Offense 1918-present	121
Chapter 14	Moving to the Modern Game – Defense 1918-present	137
Chapter 15	Epilogue	143
Appendix I	Rules	149
Appendix II	Annotated Bibliography	169
Index		179

PREFACE

Many authors have written books about the history of football; however, each one focuses on some aspect of the game, a player, a coach, or a team. Most of the famous coaches also have written their own books, but I have not found one that explains in detail exactly how the game was played and how that play changed over time. Some histories cover that topic, but only for a limited period of time or for a particular team. Others touch on it, but not in detail. My intention in this book is to allow the reader to envision just how playing the game happened step by step. We may be able to learn something from this about the creation of games and other human institutions and about why football is so popular. Of course, rules are very important. They determine how the game should be played, and, in turn, the play determines new rule changes. My attention to rules is secondary to explaining how play developed.

The discussion is centered on collegiate play and rules with occasional reference to professional football. The collegians created the game and were the primary focus of popular attention until well after World War II. The pros followed the collegiate rules until 1933. Since then there has been some divergence between college and pro, but the differences have remained fairly unimportant. Of course, we also now have flag football, high school football, pee-wee football, Warner league football, six-man football, women's football, and arena (indoor) football. The rules for each of these differ in some respect from the Nation Collegiate Athletic Association (NCAA) rules. Even the NCAA differentiates in slight ways between its various divisions, created in 1973. It would be a herculean task to try to discuss the different rules for all of these versions of the game, and, from an historical viewpoint, quite unnecessary.

A good historian would have to consult primary sources to determine his or her historical narrative. In the case of football, this means examining university archives, old rulebooks, student news outlets, old newspapers and magazines, and memoirs of players and coaches, as well as the records of organizations such as the NCAA or the professional National Football League (NFL). I have found that most of this work has already been done by the book authors in my bibliography and by others. In addition, there are now many resources available on the internet, either to read or to download. This is especially true of publications prior to 1923 which are out of copyright including photos therein. So, I have relied on all of these resources in putting my own narrative together. Where there are differences or discrepancies, I have tried to compare sources and have relied on those that appear to be the most consistent and authentic.

I want to thank Grace Capwell and Tom Herget for very valuable editorial assistance.

CHAPTER I

EARLY BEGINNINGS

1840s to 1869

An old game. On an autumn afternoon in the United States one can watch televised games of soccer, rugby, and American football. The three games are quite different; they would not be confused with one another. Yet they all have the same origins. Each developed out of a simple game involving a ball and the foot, having no official rules and a variety of styles. Records indicate that some form of a game in which a ball is kicked was played in many places around the world since ancient times.

The object was for one team to kick the ball across an imaginary line at one end of the playing area, and for the other team to kick the ball across an imaginary line at the other end of the area. The line might be defined by a fence, a sidewalk, a wall, or a space between two trees. The ball crossing the line would constitute a "goal," and the team with the most goals would win. The number of players could vary from a handful to a hundred or so. The playing area had no uniform size; it was usually as long and as wide as whatever field was available. No standard length of time for the game was settled upon. There were no codified rules; simple tradition prevailed. This kind of game is still played by youngsters in the streets of Italy, China, Argentina, and all over the world. It's a great game. All you need is a ball.

Football

English antecedents. The immediate predecessor of soccer, rugby, and American football, however, can be found in England. In that country, since at least the eighteenth century, stories are told of young men playing a game in which a ball is kicked back and forth on a field by various numbers of players. In the nineteenth century this type of game was played by students in the so-called "public" schools in England, including Charterhouse, Eton, Forrest, Rugby, Shrewsbury, Westminster, and Winchester. In spite of the name, these were actually private prep schools for the universities of Oxford and Cambridge.

The Eton School

At first all the games were intramural, that is, one school did not play against another. Rather, teams were formed within the school, and they played each other. The style of these games became embedded in tradition over time, and the rules developed differently at each school. Some of these prep school players introduced the game at the university level in 1846, and foot ball (or kick ball) was eventually played at Oxford and Cambridge also as an intramural sport. Football clubs with no school affiliation also began to form in London and other cities at this time. Beginning in the 1840's the English game had been introduced to some of the eastern universities and prep schools in the United States where it was, again, played only as an intramural sport.

Rule variations. Since schools did not play one another at this time, it was not necessary to have uniform rules for the game. In fact, there were as many variations of the "game" as there were schools and clubs. One variation, however, was especially significant. At the Rugby school in Rugby, England, the rules were changed to allow a player to catch the ball with his hands and run with it, and his opponents were allowed to tackle him. This supposedly occurred as early as 1823 when a player named William Webb Ellis, with time running out, decided to run with the ball in defiance of the rules to score a goal. After some reflection, his contemporaries apparently thought this was a good idea. Whether this is how it started or not, the players at the Rugby school were certainly playing the "carrying game" by the 1840s.

In 1857 Thomas Hughes, a former Rugby student, wrote *Tom Brown's School Days,* a fictionalized tale of his experiences at the school in which playing rugby style football was a major theme. This book proved to be very influential in America in later years. It was during this period that goal posts were introduced in various sizes and shapes in England, and at Eton the number of players on a team was fixed at eleven (although not at other schools).

Uniform rules. Some of the English footballers felt a need to codify the rules for the teams that played within their schools. Cambridge and several other schools approved eleven rules for the kicking game in 1848. Another set of eleven rules, slightly different, were written by the British Sheffield Club in 1857. The Uppingham School wrote its own set of ten rules in 1862. The Cambridge rules were revised and published in 1863. This may have been in response to a growing interest in playing inter-school or inter-club matches. In that same year a group of clubs and schools came together in London to form the London Football Association. This group, in considering adopting a uniform set of rules for the game, rejected the rugby rule permitting players to catch and run with the ball.

The teams that played the rugby style refused to go along with this decision and pulled out of the meeting. The Sheffield Club and others that played by rugby-type rules also did not join the Association. The rules that were adopted were based upon the Cambridge rules and were called the "Football Rules of the London Football Association" (see Appendix I). These rules, or something like them, were eventually adopted by teams in both England and America, and the game became known as "Association Football." It is still called that in England. Sometime in the early twentieth century the word "soccer" was used by Americans as equivalent to Association Football. The new word supposedly is a corruption of "Association," although how that worked out is not clear.

Rugby still popular. The rugby-style game was not confined to the Rugby school. It enjoyed some popularity at other schools in England, Canada, and some American prep schools. Oxford established a team in 1869. Thus, by 1870 there were two games of "foot ball" being played by the various schools and clubs. The availability of fast and low cost transportation through the relatively new English railroad network probably made the possibility of inter-school or inter-club play economically feasible. A group of students at Rugby had devised and published a set of rules for their team as early as 1845. As time passed, and transportation became available, all the English rugby teams, like the Association teams, felt the need for uniform rules to govern the game. As a result, the Rugby Football Union was organized in London in 1871 and established the "Laws of the Game of Football as Played by the Rugby Union," shortened to "Rugby Union Rules" (see Appendix I).

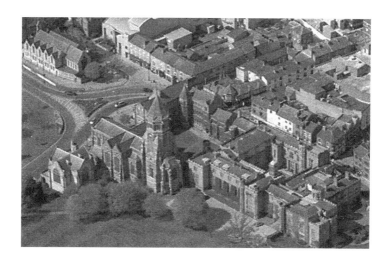

The Rugby School

American adoption of rules. Although some prep and high schools were playing rugby, the Americans playing football had generally mimicked the Association game as played in England, but each school had a slightly different version of the rules. Intercollegiate competition was finally accomplished in 1869 when Princeton (then the College of New Jersey) played Rutgers in Brunswick, New Jersey. Rutgers won, 6 to 4. A second game between the two teams was played at Princeton the following week. Score: Princeton 8, Rutgers 0. Further competition was held between these two teams and between Rutgers and Columbia in 1870.

Seeking uniformity. To resolve the problem of different rules, the practice was borrowed from intramural experience of having the captains (there were no coaches) of each team meet before the game and decide which set of rules to play under, or, alternatively, to pick and choose among those rules where there were conflicts. Preparing for further intercollegiate competition, Princeton publicly announced its code of rules in 1871. Yale and Harvard followed in 1872 by establishing university football associations ("varsities") and rules for their own game. Intercollegiate matches were held in that same year between Yale and Columbia and between Princeton and Rutgers.

Princeton asked representatives from Columbia, Rutgers, and Yale to meet with them in 1873. They adopted a uniform set of rules for play among each other (the 1873 rules). No league was formed at that time. Four games were played under those rules in 1873. More schools joined in the college competition in the 1870s, all playing some form of Association rules. In fact many teams in the mid-west and the south as well as the northeast had begun playing Association football by 1873.

"Old Nassau" (original building) on Princeton Campus

CHAPTER 2

THE ASSOCIATION GAME

1869 to 1874

A simple kicking game. Just what sort of game was it that was played by these schools and clubs in the 1860s and early 1870s? From the reports of early games and an application of the early rules we can reconstruct the play. First, it was a very simple game. The original Association rules numbered only 13. The rules adopted by the four American universities in 1873 had only 12 rules. But this is somewhat misleading. Most of the terms used in the rules were not defined, and yet they incorporated traditional meanings. For instance, one who was unfamiliar with the game would have no idea what terms like *free kick*, *in touch*, *fair catch*, or *hacking*, meant. So, to understand the rules, a player would already have to have some knowledge of the game.

The field. According to Association rules, the field on which the game was played could be a maximum of 200 yards long and 100 yards wide, the rule-makers allowing leeway for differing physical facilities. The 1873 rules (applicable only to those teams) fixed the dimensions at 400 feet by 250 feet. The corners of the field were marked off by flags, and goal posts were placed in the middle of the goal lines 25 feet apart. There was a tape between the goalposts at a height of eight feet under Association rules (added in 1866), but no such cross bar was required under the 1873 rules. A goal was scored when the ball was kicked between the goalposts. At some venues in the

1860s the field contained tree stumps, animal droppings, and low spots that would hold water or mud.

Captains and officials. Each team elected a captain who was usually an experienced and talented player. The captain would participate in the coin toss and, under rules in effect from 1871, would also participate in naming the officials. These consisted of two judges and one referee. The judges' function was to report infractions to the referee and to argue for their own team over controversial calls, thus becoming on-the-field advocates. Arguments were frequent, and arguing a point was often used as a stalling tactic. The referee made the final decisions. There were no coaches or advisers at this time, so the captains made other decisions such as whether to remove an injured player and who might substitute for that player. Once a player left the game, he could not return.

The ball. The ball used in football was originally nothing more than an inflated pig's bladder. This was far from ideal for several reasons. Pig bladders were difficult to inflate, and often deflated during a game. They were also subject to rotting. The size of the ball would vary with the size of the pig that it came from, and its shape was something like a flattened pear with some small appendages. When inflated it would approximate an oval shape. At some point, around the late 1830s, a cover for the bladder was made from cowhide strips to give it more durability. Intramural teams at Princeton began using this type of ball in 1858. Charles Goodyear, inventor of vulcanized rubber, made an all rubber football in 1855, and an Englishman by the name of H. J. Lindon invented an inflatable round rubber "bladder" in 1862. This was covered with leather and became the standard football. By the late 1860s and early 1870s all teams were using the spherical leather-covered ball, although the size was still not uniform. The 1873 rules provided that the ball should be a "number six" which meant an entirely round ball imported from England with a 30 inch circumference. This was also the ball adopted by the English Association.

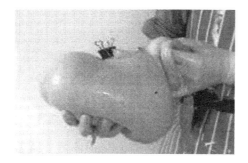
Pig's Bladder

Association Ball

Teams. The number of players on each side was not specified in the English Association rules, although the 1873 rules required 20 players on a side. Among other schools and clubs, the actual number of players varied considerably. One game between Virginia Military Institute and Washington & Lee in 1873 called for 40 players on a side. Often the number would be 15. Yale played a game with alumni of the Eton school from England in 1873, and the number of players was restricted to eleven, per Eton rules. Teams at this time wore no protective gear, including helmets, and no uniforms. Occasionally a bandana or a stocking cap, sometimes called a turban, of a certain color was worn by a team to differentiate them from their opponents.

Playing the game. The game began with a kickoff from the center of the field. The receiving team lined up at least ten yards in front of the kick. A player from that team would field the ball with his feet and begin to advance toward the opponents. No player could pick up the ball, run with it, or catch it in his hands. An exception existed among those teams recognizing the "fair catch" and "free kick" rule. This rule provided that any player could catch a kicked ball while in the air with his hands and arms, then make a mark in the turf with his heel, and then step back as far as he wanted and make his own kick without hindrance or interference from the opposing side.

The ball was usually advanced by "dribbling," also called "babying" or "puddling." This was a skillful way of manipulating the ball with the feet while controlling it. It was the major skill involved in the game.

Blocking for the dribbler. One feature of the American game at this time that did not survive in later Association football was the use of a semicircle or wedge of players on either side or behind the dribbling player. The players in the wedge would try to prevent defenders from challenging the dribbler. See the discussion of the offside rule below. The countermeasure to this tactic was to break up the wedge by charging violently and knocking down the wedge participants. This, of course, lent a dangerous feature to the game. Tempers would flare, and punching, tripping, kneeing, and other misdeeds would often occur.

More rules. If the ball went out of bounds on the sidelines (called "in touch"), it would be kicked in or tossed in, by the team that did not touch it last. If the ball went out of bounds at the goal line, it would be kicked in by the team defending that goal. Scoring was usually by counting each goal (variously called "games," or "innings,") as one point. Some games were ended by a time limit, up to three or more hours in some cases, or by reaching a total number of goals – six was often the number. The rules provided for no fouls or referees until 1871, and even then no penalties. This reflected the idea that football was a "gentleman's game" and that gentlemen would not be unsportsmanlike and infringe the rules. There was no "possession" of the ball by either team, although a good dribbler could control the ball for many seconds and might pass (by kicking) to a teammate.

Field position. Of course, the positioning of the players on the field would vary with the number of players. In general, a few players were placed back to protect their goal. One in particular was designated to stand at the goal itself – the goalkeeper. A larger number of players occupied the center of the field, and they moved back and forth with the ball, more or less, either to defend or to advance the ball toward the opponent's goal. A third and smaller group could be stationed around the opponent's goal if the rules for the particular game did not have an "offside" provision. The concept of offside was very controversial in both England and America.

The offside problem. The tradition among some teams in England was to place players with special kicking skills near the opponent's goal. These would receive passes (by kicking) from other players and kick the ball through the goal. However, another tradition, perhaps adhered to by a larger number of teams, held that such "goal hanging" distorted the game, and the use of such goal hangers was unfair. This group made the goal hanger illegal with the offside rule.

There were actually two kinds of offside rules which might be called the "hard" and the "soft" versions. The hard version did not permit any player to get between the ball and the opponent's goal. As the ball was advanced down the field by the attacking team, no player on that team was allowed to venture into this forbidden territory. If he did, he was "offside." An offside player was considered out of the game. He could not kick or touch the ball, touch any other player, or actively participate in the game. However, an offside player could become "onside" if the ball passed him (putting him back behind the ball) or if an opponent touched the ball. The hard version was adopted in the 1863 Association rules and eventually worked its way into the rules of rugby.

The soft version of the offside rule allowed a player to get ahead of the ball, provided that there were at least three players of the opposite team between him and the opponent's goal (including goalie). In 1866 the English Association changed from the hard to the soft version and also allowed goalies to catch the ball with their hands.

Effect of the offside rule. For teams that played by the offside rule, the ball could be passed, by kick, from one player to another, but the pass had to be lateral or backward. Thus, the progress of the ball toward the opponent's goal was made by moving forward dribbling and passing sideways or backwards as the situation warranted. A pass in the forward direction would normally be intercepted by one of the opposing players, but it could be successfully made to a teammate if that player came up quickly from behind the ball to receive it. Forming a human barrier or wedge around the dribbler was limited to runners on the sides and at the rear of the dribbler because players in front of the dribbler would be ahead of the ball and hence offside. So, the wedge tactic was only mildly effective. For games played without the offside rule, players could pass the ball (by kick) forward to teammates in front of them, and a wedge completely surrounding the dribbler could be used. Under the soft version of the offside rule, some use of the wedge and some forward passing (by kick) were possible.

Americans and the offside rule. While the American teams playing the Association game generally adopted the 1863 Association rules, they did so with some editing. If we look closely at the record, it would appear that the offside rule was not popular on this side of the Atlantic. In the first American intercollegiate game (Princeton-Rutgers 1869) we find that the offside rule was not followed. In his description of the game, historian Parke H. Davis tells us: "Two men were stationed by each team to play immediately in front of the opponents' goal and were known as captains of the enemy's goal." Such positioned players were also used by the Sheffield teams in England and were called "kick throughs." Davis also tells us that the ball was moved by the dribbler with "the other players surrounding the ball and not permitting a Princeton man to get near it." Of course, neither of these practices would be allowed if the offside rule were in effect. Neither the Princeton rules of 1871 nor the Yale rules of 1872 contained an offside rule. The same is true of the 1873 rules adopted by Princeton, Rutgers, Columbia and Yale. A few American club teams played by the Sheffield rules at this time which also ignored the offside concept.

Summary of play. So what kind of a game do we have here? Again, it's very simple. The ball is kicked off, then back and forth; players try to advance it by dribbling. The wedge tactic is used when feasible, and, presumably because of this, the American game is considered "rough" by observers. Some passing between attacking players occurs. Defenders try to disrupt the dribbler and obtain the ball (but no use of hands or arms). Long kicks toward the opponents' goal are made when the dribbler gets in trouble. Goals are kicked in from any distance, but are more likely to be successful if kicked from a short distance. Does this strangely sound like the game of soccer played around the world in the twenty-first century? It is, of course, essentially the same with two major differences: 1) the offside rule (soft version) is still in effect today, and 2) penalty kicks are now provided for fouls.

CHAPTER 3

THE SHORT TRANSITION: ASSOCIATION TO RUGBY

1874 to 1876

Harvard gets rough. The record of football at Harvard before 1858 is very sketchy. It is possible that Association style games were played in the 1840s and 1850s, but a form of rugby is more likely. One tradition was the annual freshman-sophomore game. It was called by some, at Harvard and other schools, the "class rush." This spectacle in 1858 is reported as an important social event which drew quite a crowd. It involved large numbers of both classes, perhaps more than 100 on a side, squaring off in two lines.

The game was started when the team with the ball, the freshmen, tried to penetrate the sophomore line of defense by having one of their largest men run with the ball. He would be assisted by other big men trying to run interference. If there were rules, they were mostly disregarded. The whole affair was more of a hazing of freshmen by the sophomores, and it occasionally got rough. The intramural games played in that year were more gentle in nature. The next year followed the same pattern, and the freshman-sophomore matchup was again a big social event. But the rough play resulted in many injuries, some serious, and the game came to be known as "Bloody Monday."

Harvard drops out. The violence and resulting injuries of the freshman-sophomore game in 1859 induced the Harvard administration and faculty to outlaw the game of football in the spring of 1860. Many of the students were opposed to this, but they acquiesced. They staged an elaborate "funeral" for poor old football with a grave, mourners, and a touching eulogy. Although an attempt was made to revive the game on campus in 1864, it failed. The prohibition of any kind of football at Harvard lasted until 1871.

Importance of abolishing football. If Harvard had not prohibited football for 10 years, the game of American football as we know it may never have developed. It seems very likely that Harvard would have begun playing the Association game along with its fellow ivy-leaguers. If that happened, the Boston Rules game (see below) would never have been created. There were certainly no influences to play rugby in the 1860s as there were in the 1870s. Given Harvard's big role in bringing rugby to the college campuses, rugby might never have been adopted, and everyone would still be playing Association football. It is possible that other teams playing the rugby game, perhaps in the Chicago area, might have formed a league or a rule-making body that could lead to further development. Whether that would lead to a new game, American football, as it actually did with the ivy-leaguers, seems highly unlikely.

Play by Boston high schools. The preparatory schools in the Boston area continued to play football after Harvard's exit in 1860. Pick-up games were frequent on the Boston Commons. Some players competed in interscholastic games. These involved the Dixwell Latin School, the Boston Public Latin School, the Roxbury Latin School, the Dorchester High School, and the Phillips Academy of Andover. The Dixwell Latin School was dominant, and in 1862 a club team was formed of Dixwell players and a few from other teams. They called their club the "Oneidas" after a long-vanished Indian tribe of the area. The Oneidas played all comers, including alumni teams, and combined teams of players from other schools; they even challenged the freshmen at Harvard in 1864, but the game was not played. Not only was the Oneida club never defeated, but it was never scored upon.

As students drifted away over time, the club dissolved. Toward the end of the decade pick-up games were still being played in the Boston Commons.

Ball Won by Oneida Football Club

The Boston Rules. These young high schoolers did not play the Association game or rugby. They worked out their own brand of football which came to be called the "Boston Game" or the "Boston Rules Game" by journalists of the time. It differed from Association football in that players could run with the ball and be tackled by opponents. It differed from rugby in that there was no scrummage and no touchdown. The number of players varied from 10 to 17. The goals were the imaginary lines at the ends of the field – no goal posts of any kind. To score a goal, the ball had to be kicked over the line. There was no half-time and no rests after a goal was scored. The ball was constantly moving unless play was stopped when the ball went out of bounds. Free kicks were used, and the ball could be passed from one player to another using the hands.

Play at the Boston Commons

More rules. Author John D. Lovett, himself one of the Oneida players, tells us of another practice that raises intriguing questions. He recalls, "Beebe, with body bent close to the ground, [was] patting the ball with his hands, this way and that, steering it clear of the ravening wolves who were pursuing and rapidly hemming him in." Like dribbling a basketball?

The Boston game recognized an offside rule of sorts. If a player strayed into the area near the opponent's goal (ahead of the ball, of course), it was called "lurking" and was regarded as unsportsmanlike. The defender nearest his own goal line was called the "tender out," similar to a goalie, but without goal posts. He had to defend the whole line. The term "goal" was not used to mean a score; that was called a "game." Usually two out of three "games" would decide the match. Finally, one other strange rule should be mentioned. Ball carriers could not be tackled unless they were moving toward the opponent's goal. How this rule worked remains a mystery. The Boston Rules were apparently never written down; they were simply a matter of tradition. Soon the tradition moved to the university.

Harvard's return. In 1871, succumbing to student pressure, the Harvard administration decided to permit football once again. Several intramural games were played in the spring and fall of 1872. Probably due to the influence of some former Boston area prep school graduates who had become Harvard students, the game that was played was the Boston Rules game. There was apparently no inclination to institute the Association game. In 1872 Association style games were played between Yale and Columbia and between Princeton and Rutgers. As outlined above, in 1873 these same schools met to adopt uniform rules. Harvard was invited to participate, but declined on the grounds that its style of play, Boston Rules, was too different to be assimilated to the Association game.

This left Harvard with no one to play on an intercollegiate level, so the Boston game continued only at an intramural level. Then, in 1874 an invitation to competition came from an unexpected source: McGill University of Montreal, Canada. The Canadians challenged Harvard to a series of football games. McGill played under the all-Canada rules which were a slightly modified version of Rugby Union rules. One important feature that differed from the English game was that touchdowns were counted in the scoring.

Rugby gets established. Three games resulted from this challenge, the first two played in Cambridge. Harvard (Boston) rules were used in the first match played on May 14, 1874, but the second game a day later came under rugby rules. Harvard won the first 3 - 0, and the second ended in a scoreless tie. The third game, again rugby, was played in Montreal in October of the same year. Harvard won 3 touchdowns to none. Apparently unnoticed, the New Brunswick, New Jersey, newspaper reported a game of rugby between Rutgers and Columbia in November of 1872.

Harvard v. McGill, Jarvis Field, Cambridge, Mass. 1874

Significance of Harvard-McGill. If the Harvard-McGill games had not been played, it appears that Association football would have remained the dominant game in America. Without McGill, Harvard would have been left with no collegiate teams to compete with, and would have had no exposure to the rugby game. Harvard was competitive with ivy-league schools in other sports, so it seems likely that the Crimson would have come around to Association ball. There is no indication that other schools were interested in the Boston game, and, indeed, competition in the Association game was on the upswing.

One other important consequence of the McGill-Harvard games is that counting touchdowns in the scoring was brought to American rugby. So, if those games had not been played, and rugby was somehow eventually adopted, the game would probably follow the English lead in counting only goals in scoring. This, in itself, could have had quite an impact on the

American game. The scoring of touchdowns emphasized the running game and downplayed the kicking game.

In the meantime, students from Tufts College who had witnessed the earlier Harvard-McGill matches began practicing the rugby game and challenged Harvard to a match that took place in June of 1875. Tufts upset the Harvard Crimson 1 goal, 1 touchdown to nothing. This is sometimes considered the first intercollegiate rugby game between teams in the United States. But, did the Rutgers/Columbia game mentioned above actually occur? Harvard again played Tufts in the fall of 1875 as well as a Canadian club composed of players from different schools. Club teams in Chicago also began playing rugby at this time.

Yale and concessionary rules. Yale and Harvard had a rivalry in baseball and other sports, so it was perhaps inevitable that football should be included. The Harvardians thought that their new rugby game was superior to the Association game and wanted to demonstrate it to the Elis (Yale students). Yale agreed to the match, but demanded certain concessions. Yale insisted that only goals should count as scores and touchdowns should not; they also insisted on using and all-rubber ball. Although Yale wanted 11 men on a side (experience with Eton), they conceded to Harvard's 15. Other minor modifications were made, but the game was primarily rugby. It was played on November 15, 1875. As might be expected, Harvard won 4 to 0, mainly due to Yale's inexperience in dealing with the running and tackling game. A crowd of 2,000 watched the match. They were treated to quite a spectacle as both teams wore uniforms for the first time – called "costumes" then. Observers from Princeton were present, and they reported back to their colleagues that the new game had great appeal.

Rugby spreads. At this point a truly unusual phenomenon began. Suddenly rugby became the game to play. A number of teams abandoned their Association game and decided to play rugby instead, although a few schools continued both styles of football. In 1876 teams from Columbia, Harvard, Princeton, Stevens Tech, Tufts, Yale, and a group of Canadian all-stars played intercollegiate games of rugby. Also, in the Chicago area college and club teams played against each other. Historian Melvin I. Smith has calculated that in 1875 39 teams were playing the Association game and nine were playing rugby. By 1878 there were 21 Association teams and 52 rugby teams. Why this change occurred so quickly remains a mystery. Some historians have suggested that the influence of the book, *Tom Brown's School Days,* was a prime factor. But the timing is not right. That book was first published in 1857 and had run through multiple editions by 1875. Why should it suddenly have an influence in the late 1870s?

The IFA and uniform rules. As it had done with Association football, Princeton again led the way toward establishing uniform rules. In late November of 1876 Princeton invited Columbia, Harvard, and Yale to a meeting in Springfield, Massachusetts, to consider uniform rules for the rugby game. Student delegates represented each of the schools. They formed a new league called the Intercollegiate Football Association (IFA), sometimes called the American Intercollegiate Football Association. Yale declined to join the league formally at this time, but participated anyway. The group essentially adopted the 59 Rugby Union Rules of 1871 word-for-word with a few exceptions. Although not in the rules, the IFA decided to recommend use of the Number 5 leather rugby ball used in England. This ball had a short circumference of 27 to 28 inches.

Eight of the rules were slightly reworded or had language added for clarification. Three more simply changed the reference to other rule numbers. Rule 59 was changed to provide for two judges and a referee instead of having the captains decide disputes. Rules 60 and 61 were added to make the size of the field 140 yards by 70 yards and to limit the number of players on a side to 15. One other change of importance was Rule seven. The Rugby Union Rules provided that a match was decided by a majority of (kicked) goals. The Americans, borrowing from the Canadians, thought that the touchdown was important enough to count in the scoring. They came up with the following: *Rule 7. A match shall be decided by a majority of touchdowns; a goal shall be equal to four touchdowns; but in case of a tie, a goal kicked from a touchdown shall take precedence over four touchdowns.* This scoring formulation, confusing as it was, did not last, and has been changed 11 times since. Games were played under these rules without modification for three years.

CHAPTER 4

THE RUGBY GAME

1876 to 1880

A complicated game. Unlike the Association game with its 13 rules, the American rugby game had 61 rules to make a more complicated form of football. There were, of course, many similarities. Two judges were provided who had the same advocacy function as in Association football. A lone referee was supposed to enforce the rules. Goal posts were required, but they were different from Association goalposts. The posts were to be 18 ½ feet apart with a crossbar 10 feet above the ground, however, the kick had to go over the cross bar rather than under it (as in Association football). This led to different types of kicking: the drop kick, the place kick, and the punt. The size of the field was fixed at 110 yards in length and 53 1/3 yards in width. The posts were on the goal line, not behind it. There was no end zone as such, simply space behind the goal posts. There were offside rules in both games.

The ball. The ball used in rugby was oblong, shaped about the size of a watermelon. How this came about is a mystery. Some have thought that the shape of the pig's bladder determined the shape of the ball, but the pig's bladder does not correspond very closely to the watermelon even when inflated. And, those early teams in England playing the kicking game (later, Association) succeeded in using a spherical ball with the same pig's bladder.

The Rugby ball.

Others have suggested that a drop kick, used in rugby, but not in Association, can be more easily executed with an oblong ball than with a round ball. This is highly doubtful. Finally, it has been claimed that the oblong ball rather than the round ball can be carried and secured more easily by a runner. This is possible but debatable. We do know that the shape of the ball was determined before the rubber bladder came on the scene. In later years the official rules described the ball as a "prolate spheroid," as if that explained everything.

Teams. Fifteen men on a side constituted a team. They wore no protective gear, but uniforms (called "costumes" then) did appear in this period. In the Harvard-Yale game of 1875 Harvard appeared in crimson uniforms, and Yale wore yellow caps, blue shirts, and dark trousers. Later in 1879 Princeton set a style by wearing orange and black striped jerseys (tigers, of course) under sleeveless canvas jackets. Earlier, the Eton and McGill teams had also worn uniforms,. None of these outfits contained any padding. Helmets were not worn. On the field the players were roughly divided into forwards and backs, although this was not a requirement of the rules. The forwards were usually the bulky strong men, and the backs were agile speedy types. The forwards pushed in the scrummage, and the backs ran and passed, and they were also required to play back defensively to receive kicks.

Running and tackling. A player was allowed to run with the ball, and his opponents could tackle him. A tackle was originally called a "maul" at the Rugby School. The rule against tripping was interpreted to include tripping by hand so that tackling was required to be above the waist. This meant that a runner could continue running even though a tackler or two, or three, had grabbed him. A strong heavy runner with good balance could add quite a few yards to his gain while being tackled. When he was finally knocked down, he could still crawl forward to gain yardage, and his teammates were allowed to push him as well. He could also try to pass the ball to a teammate while being tackled or on the ground. The ball was not dead until the carrier touched it to the ground and yelled "down!"

Maul in goal. A particularly violent sort of tackling occurred with what was called "maul in goal." A touchdown was not scored until the ball had been touched down behind the opponent's goal line. Therefore, a ball carrier could be tackled as he was crossing the goal line or after he had crossed the goal line as long as he had not touched the ball down. When this happened several opponents would try to prevent him from touching the ball down and to grab the ball away from him. It became quite a wrestling match with players of both sides punching the ball and sometimes punching each other. If the defense succeeded in taking the ball from the carrier, they could down it for a touchback.

The scrummage. The scrummage (often called a scrum) is the most unique feature of rugby. It is a method of putting the ball in play after a runner has been downed or sometimes after the ball has gone out of bounds (called "in touch"). Several members of both teams, usually nine or ten on a side, line up facing each other along an imaginary line running parallel to the goal lines through the point where the ball is to be placed down. The scrummagers take up a squatting position with arms intertwined, some of them in back of the first line to give support and help push. The player who had been downed (later, the referee) rolls the ball in between the opposing sides to start the play. Both sides then push against each other in an attempt to move the ball in the direction of the opponent's goal. Those participating in the scrummage cannot touch the ball with their hands. They try to move it with their feet. Other players stand in back of the scrummage ready to pick up the ball when and if it squirts out of the scrummage line.

If this happens, the player picking up the ball can run with it, pass it backwards to a teammate, or kick it. If team A is successful in pushing back team B, the ball can be kicked forward, bit by bit, for more pushing, thus improving field position, or it can be kicked backward ("heeled") out of the scrummage to a waiting back. Because of the number of players on each side all kicking and pushing, the outcome of the scrummage is usually in doubt. One side or the other may get the ball. The scrummage serves a function analogous to that of a jump ball in basketball.

The Scrummage

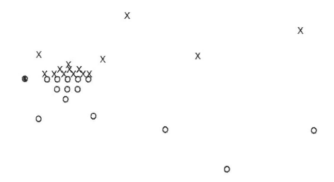

Position of players in the scrummage

An actual scrummage on the Rugby grounds.

Kicking. A place kick is used to start each half of the game and to start play after a goal has been made. In this case it is called a kick-off. It can also be used to kick a goal. The ball may be held by a player other than the kicker or it may be placed in a small depression in the turf without being held. When a goal has been scored, the team that lost the goal is the team that kicks off. A drop kick can be used to score a goal as well. The drop kick is executed by the kicker dropping the ball. After it hits the ground, it is immediately kicked as it starts to bounce back up. The kicker makes a punt by dropping the ball from his hands and kicking it before it touches the ground. A punt can be made any time (other than during a scrummage), but punting cannot score a goal. Players often punt on the run.

The punt is an effective means of advancing the ball down the field, sometimes more effective than a run. This is because of what happens when a tackle is made. For example, if a player runs with the ball for 20 yards and is tackled, a scrummage results at that point, and possession of the ball will be anyone's guess. If he punts the ball 40 yards, and it is fielded by an opponent who is immediately tackled, again you have a scrummage and possession is in question. But the punt has netted 40 yards in field position while the run has only resulted in a 20-yard gain.

Fair catch, free kick. As in Association football, a player may catch a kick on the fly and then make a free kick. After the catch he makes a mark in the field with his heel. He then steps back as far as he deems necessary and kicks the ball. The opponents must not come closer to the kicker than the mark on the turf, and the kicker's teammates must stand behind him until the kick is made. The kick may be a punt, drop kick, or place kick.

Preparing for Free Kick

Offside. Rugby follows a hard offside rule. This means that the players of each team must remain behind the ball, that is, between the ball and their own goal. A player becomes onside when the ball passes him, when it touches an opponent, or when an opponent has run with the ball five yards. The rule applies to the scrummage as well, and both sides must stay between the ball and their own goal. As in Association football, offside has its greatest effect on the passing game. The ball may be passed with hands and arms from one player to another, but all passes must be lateral or backwards.

In touch. The rules that apply when the ball goes out of bounds, called "in touch," are more complicated. If the ball goes out of bounds from a kick or a pass, it is awarded to the player who recovers it out of bounds and touches it down. This means that there will usually be a big scramble off the field for the loose ball. If a ball carrier steps out of bounds, he retains possession of the ball. The person entitled to possession then has three options to put the ball back in play. With both teams standing on their respective sides of the ball, he may 1) bounce the ball onto the field and attempt to grab possession of it and then run, kick, or pass, or 2) he may throw the ball straight out at right angles to the sideline, or 3) he may walk it out no less than five yards nor more than 15 yards and place it down there. If this method is chosen, a scrummage would follow.

Scoring. In the American rugby game during the late 1870s scoring was also somewhat complicated (see IFA scoring rules above). A goal was scored when a place kick or drop kick went between the goalposts and over the cross bar. This was normally executed from a free kick. A touchdown (also called a "run in") was scored when a ball carrier crossed the opponent's goal line and touched the ball down. Making a touchdown allowed a team a "try at goal." Here the point at which the runner touched the ball down became important. From that point the ball could be taken out perpendicular to the goal line to any distance satisfactory to the team that scored the touchdown and there kicked by place kick or drop kick (essentially a free kick) for a goal. The kicker's team had to remain behind the ball, and the other team had to remain behind their goal line until the ball was kicked.

The Place Kick

The punt out. If the ball had been downed close to the goal posts, marching it out a few yards for a place kick would work well. However, if the touchdown were scored near the sidelines, this would create an angle that made it difficult for the kicker. In that case, if the ball were brought out only a few yards, the angle of the kick would be too great. On the other hand, if the ball were brought out a long distance, the angle decreased, but the distance to the goalposts increased. This is where the "punt out" came in. The team scoring the touchdown, instead of bringing the ball straight out, could choose to punt the ball from the goal line to a teammate. The opponents could not obstruct this punter, standing on the goal line in front of the spot where the ball had been touched down. He would punt the ball to his teammate standing in front of the goalposts, the teammate would make a fair catch, and then the drop kick or place kick would be made as before.

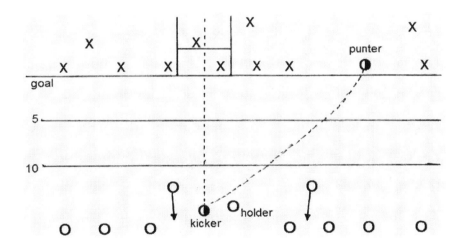

Punt out. Punter punts to kicker who drop kicks or place kicks for goal.

This assumes, of course, that all went well. Sometimes the fair catch was not made, and at other times either the punt or the kick would go awry. Then the goal failed, and this put the ball in play again. As the IFA rule above stated, both goals and touchdowns counted in determining who won the match. For example, in 1876 Yale beat Princeton 2 goals, 2 touchdowns to 0, and also beat Columbia 2 goals, 5 touchdowns to 1 touchdown. Use of point equivalents had to wait until 1883.

Summary of play. American rugby was a rowdy game with lots of running, passing, and kicking. The "wedge" type of running interference for the ball carrier was often used. Tackling and wrestling for the ball after tackling were rough features of the game with the maul in goal being the most notorious. When the ball was downed, the scrummage (jump ball) followed. The principal skills were running with the ball, passing, and kicking the different types of kick. There were no set plays or formations (except the scrummage) that would allow any kind of tactics or team play, although patterns of passing the ball laterally were followed. The scoring system, with the touchdown added, was generally unsatisfactory.

CHAPTER 5

MOVING AWAY FROM RUGBY

1880 to 1883

Gradual change. The American football that we know today grew out of the rugby game. It developed in two ways: incremental rule changes, beginning in 1880, and the changing practices or innovations by the players themselves.

In this process several factors influenced the rule changes. First, it was thought that the game could be improved. This sometimes meant that the game should allow for more strategy or "scientific" development in the form of planned attack or defense including the use of teamwork, power and deception. Improvement of the game perhaps more often simply meant correcting the unforeseen consequences of earlier rule adoptions. Then it could also mean making the game more "open," favoring lateral passing and open field runs as opposed to power plays through the line. In the decade after 1900, improvement most often meant changes to reduce injuries.

The player (and later coach) innovations, sometimes in direct conflict with the rules, were motivated simply by a desire to beat the opponents. Of course, other teams inevitably copied any successful innovation.

Rule-making authority. One of the strangest features of this great transition from rugby to American football was the constitution of the rule-making authority. Unlike the situation in England in which both the Football Association and the Rugby Union provided uniform rules of play with both groups represented by many teams throughout that country, the American game for many years was in the hands of a small handful of players and ex-players from four or five elite schools (the IFA). Yet there were more than fifty schools and clubs playing the game in 1880, including some in the south, the mid-west, and the west coast.

Walter Camp. One of those rule-makers was Walter Chauncey Camp. Camp had played as an outstanding halfback at Yale beginning in 1876. Eligibility requirements were lax. Camp played four years as an undergraduate and another one and one half years as a medical student (he was injured in that sixth year). Although he became a successful businessman, Camp continued his interest in both Yale and football. He became one of the Yale representatives at the IFA meeting in 1878 and continued in this capacity for years to come. He was actually involved in football rule-making every year until his death in 1925, ironically, at a meeting of the rules committee. More importantly, with some exceptions, it was Camp who proposed many of the rules that substantially changed the game: hence, his standing as the "father of football."

Walter Camp

Unlike most of his fellow rule-makers in the early years, Camp had a vision of football as a "scientific" game. His use of the word "scientific" would not be accepted today, but it is clear what he had in mind. He saw the game as one of planning, designing, practicing, executing, and correcting. For Camp, luck was the enemy. Nothing should be left to luck. The team that wins should be the team that plays better than its opponent. As he said in 1896, "Football games are not won or lost by luck, except in very rare instances." Interestingly, the great innovative coaches – Amos Alonzo Stagg, Henry L. Williams, Fielding Yost, John Heisman, and Percy Haughton -- seemed to share some of his vision of the game. For instance, Haughton said, "[F]ootball is nothing more than a somewhat complicated game of human chess."

Players pushing the envelope. The first three changes in the rugby game, apart from counting touchdowns in the score, were brought about by the players and later either confirmed or prohibited by the rules. These were: the snap-back, running interference, and inch-kicking.

The snap-back. In the rugby period (1874-1880) players participating in the scrummage had become very skillful at kicking the ball behind them to waiting backs. At first players kicked with the heel, but it was later found that a method of snapping the ball with the toe was more effective. As time passed the main objective of the scrummage morphed from pushing the other team and the ball down the field to snapping it back for a teammate to run, pass, or kick. Both teams would develop players with this skill, and some were better than others. However, even a team with a very skilled snapper might lose the ball in a scrummage because he would not be in exactly the right position or because the ball was first kicked by the other team or because the ball bounced off the foot or leg of another scrummager. The main purpose of the scrummage had changed, but the outcome was still in question.

Running interference. Princeton introduced the idea of running interference (originally called "guarding") for the ball carrier in 1879, and Yale soon followed. This meant that players would be placed alongside the runner to block or "interfere" with tacklers. They could not be placed in front of the runner because of the offside rule, but this may have been more theoretical than actual since the lone official had difficulty enforcing this and other rules. At this time interfering could include shoving and pushing. Rugby purists considered this as unsportsmanlike; however, it was not addressed by the rules. Since this type of blocking proved effective, it was, of course, picked up by other teams, and its importance was later magnified as so-called "mass plays" were developed.

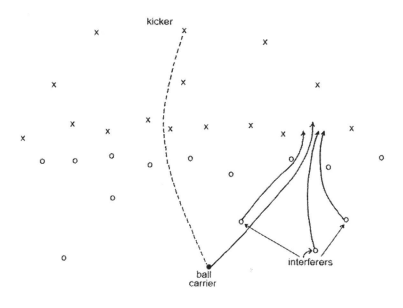

Running Interference in Rugby

If the Rugby Union rules had specifically prohibited running interference, things might have turned out quite differently. Assuming that such a rule would have been enforced by the lone official, it seems likely that the use of interference as the game progressed would not have taken place, or else a rule change would have been made. However, considering how everyone ignored the very clear offside rule (explained below), it's possible that such a rule prohibiting interference might well have been ignored too. As it turns out, the rugby interference was a precursor to the kind of interference that was used in a few years to create mass plays. Mass plays, in turn, almost brought about the downfall of football. Without interference, runners would have to rely on dodging and lateraling the football.

Inch-kicking. Sometime in the rugby period a practice developed that was technically within the rules, but actually violated them. This was what was called "inch-kicking," "babying" or "touch-off." It was used on kick-offs and kick-outs. Kick-offs, of course, were used to start each half and after a goal had been scored. Kick-outs were used after a safety was made, or, in the quaint language of the times, when a player had "touched the ball down" in his own goal.

The kicker could kick the ball robustly down the field, and in some circumstances this would be the right strategy. However, he could also tap the ball with his toe, and after it traveled an inch or even less, he could pick it up and run with it. This allowed the kicking team to keep possession of the ball when it was supposed to go to the opponents. As historian Parke H. Davis, writing in 1926, explained, "Unlike today, however, the kick-off was not required to be kicked at least 10 yards forward. The player of 1880 might, if he chose, drive the ball far down the field or, technically kicking the ball by merely touching it with his toe, he might pick it up and run with it."

The 1880 rules. Walter Camp had suggested some rule changes at the IFA meetings in 1878 and 1879 held at Springfield, Massachusetts. The group voted down all new proposals, but at the 1880 meeting Camp had more success. This meeting was held on October 12. Six rules were passed, two of them very important. *The number of players on a side was reduced from fifteen to eleven.* Yale had advocated this measure ever since their experience playing with the Eton alumni in 1874. Camp was finally able to persuade the delegates from Harvard, Princeton and Columbia that this was the right number for a team. The second major rule was even more significant. It changed the scrummage to the scrimmage. Camp's thinking, joined by others on the committee, was that the unpredictable outcome of the scrummage simply made no sense. Nor did it allow for any use of planning ahead, teamwork, or tactics. But if a team could control the ball and set play in motion, a rational attack could be planned in advance and then executed.

The scrimmage. The new rule read: *A scrimmage takes place when the holder of the ball, being in the field of play, puts it down on the ground in front of him and puts it in play while onside, first, by kicking the ball; second, by snapping it back with his foot. The man who receives the ball from the snap-back shall be called the quarterback, and shall not then rush forward with the ball under penalty of foul.* This new concept allowed a team to retain possession of the ball. Previously, after a tackle, the scrummage literally put the ball up for grabs. Now, after a tackle, the side whose player was tackled would be allowed to keep it by means of the snap-back.

Walter Camp called the new procedure "the outlet of the scrimmage." The rule also designated two players with special functions: the snapper-back and the quarterback. Since the quarterback was prohibited from running forward, he would have to hand off or pass the ball to one of the other running backs. This made possible all sorts of play combinations. It meant that plays could be drawn up in advance and practiced. The former scrummage participants, known as rushers, were eventually called linemen. The word "scrimmage" had been used by Americans for several years as a local variant on "scrummage;" the new rule made the change official.

Alternatives to scrummage and scrimmage? If the scrimmage rule had not been adopted, rugby would probably have continued in much the same form that has survived to the present day. That is what happened to Rugby Union football in England. Most of the American football rule changes that followed would make no sense without the scrimmage. It is possible, however, that some other rule could have been adopted to remedy what was seen as the pointlessness of the scrimmage.

For instance, after a tackle, the player tackled might be given a free kick. Or, a rule might have stated that after a tackle was made and the ball downed, it would be placed on the field at the point where it was downed, and the player tackled could then, without interruption from opponents and without a scrimmage, boot the ball backward to a teammate. This was the solution (called "play-the-ball") arrived at some years later in the Rugby League form of English rugby. Or, possibly a rule would allow the tackled player to pick up the ball after it had been placed down, and run with it. A neutral zone of anywhere from one to ten yards would probably be required under this hypothetical, but the idea of a neutral zone was nothing new. Although the spacing required was not called a neutral zone, such a stand-back was mandated when a free kick was made. Under this hypothetical rule, the team in possession would line up behind the person picking up the ball (the picker?) because of the offside rule, and he could pass it back to other players. The game then would continue as in normal rugby. Whether such a hypothetical practice would provide the opportunity to devise specific plays using teamwork is an open question. With such alternatives available, did Walter Camp make the right choice?

The snap-back. Originally players executed the snap-back with the foot as it had been in rugby. But the players working with the new scrimmage scheme began to "steady" the ball with the hand, and officials did not object, although this was directly in contravention of rule 14 of the original Rugby Union rules. Then they began to "guide" the snap-back with the hands. Finally, by 1890 players were using only their hands for the snap-back. Again, officials found no objection. This was another case of player innovation with no rule changes.

The original snapback from scrimmage

In making the snap-back, the ball was rolled back to the quarterback either on its long axis (on the laces) or end over end, and the quarterback had to retrieve it from the ground. In 1893, coach John Heisman invented the direct pass from the center through the air. This more efficient method was immediately adopted by other teams. Much later, in 1930, coach Ralph Jones of the Chicago Bears perfected the hand-to-hand pass from center to quarterback where the latter places his hands in the center's crotch.

Ready for the snap-back

No neutral zone. There was no neutral zone at the line of scrimmage. That imaginary line was regarded as passing through the center of the ball as it lay on the field. This meant that the lineman opposing the center (snapper-back) could touch the ball and make it difficult to snap back. This was a minor but continuing problem with the new scrimmage until it was finally outlawed. The lack of a neutral zone also meant that the opposing linemen literally stood toe to toe. They would often slap and slug each other when they could get away with it. The linemen did not assume a three or four point stance, but stood straight up.

Formations and plays. With the new scrimmage rule a standard formation on offense was developed, and plays were devised to put the ball in play. The quarterback would, of course, stand behind the snapper-back at a distance of two to five feet. He would shout out the signals to the rest of the team, indicating what play should be executed. The halfbacks stood a yard or two behind the quarterback on each side, and the fullback was in the middle another yard or so back. The halfbacks were usually the runners, and the fullback was the kicker.

The arrangement was symmetrical so that there was a threat of running the ball either to the left or the right. The positions of the linemen were gradually given names, although this was not official. They too were lined up symmetrically. Typical plays included quarterback passing to halfback who ran around end, quarterback handing off to halfback going through the line, and quarterback pitching to fullback who kicked. As time went on formations began to vary and plays became more complicated and sophisticated. On defense backs originally played at some distance behind the line to field kicks, but over time there was a tendency to move backs into the line or into a position we now call linebacker.

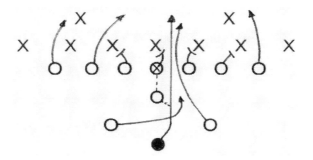

Regular Formation: Fullback plunge. Right half runs interference. QB and left half push.

The Regular Formation

The first block game. While the new scrimmage introduced the possibility of interesting and clever plays, an unforeseen development occurred that brought the new rule into question. In 1880 Princeton played Yale in their annual Thanksgiving Day game in New York City before a large crowd of 4,000. The first half had been a close dual with neither team able to score. In the second half Princeton received the ball and held on to it for the entire half without scoring. The reason for Princeton's strategy was to claim the IFA championship based on the overall season record. Taking into account the results of other league games, the tie would accordingly place Princeton ahead of the competition.

Princeton was able to retain possession of the ball for the entire half by using safeties. Under the prevailing rules a safety did not count in scoring; it simply led to a kick-out at the 25-yard line. But such a kick would normally be an "inch-kick," thus allowing the team that made the safety to retain possession. When Yale pushed the Princeton team back near its goal line, a Princeton player would run the ball back past his own goal line and down it. The final outcome was Princeton 11 safeties, Yale 6 safeties: score 0 – 0. This problem of one-possession play suggested that the new scrimmage rule could potentially seriously undermine the game of football.

The 1881 rules. Further games were played in the following year – 1881 --without the one-possession problem recurring before the IFA met again in October. At that meeting several minor rules were passed as well as one that changed the scoring. That rule provided: *In case of a tie two innings of fifteen minutes shall be played, with an interval of five minutes, the game to be decided on even innings. In case of a tie a goal kicked from a touchdown shall take precedence over a goal otherwise kicked. If the game still remains a tie, the side which makes four or more safeties less than their opponents shall win the game.* So, in this obtuse way, safeties did enter into the scoring, something that Walter Camp had advocated since 1879. Under this rule Yale would have won the previous year's game instead of ending in a tie. It is not clear whether the rule was aimed at the one-possession problem or simply at the problem of tie games.

The second block game. Either way, Princeton ingenuity managed to circumvent the new rule. At the Thanksgiving Day game in New York in 1881, a month after the IFA meeting on rules, Princeton managed to keep the ball the entire first half, and Yale did the same thing in the second half. Score: 0 – 0. Attended by a crowd of 10,000 disappointed fans, this became known as the "block" game. The reason for playing for a tie was again to win the IFA championship, although the calculations of the two schools on this matter obviously differed.

But an even more important factor became obvious; any team that was ahead in a game could use the one-possession trick to win. Once ahead, they could simply sit on the ball and let the time run out. The method by which the safety rule was circumvented in the second block game was by touching down the ball in the touch-in-goal instead of in goal. Touch-in-goal was that space behind the goal line and outside the touch (out of bounds) sideline. Touching down in that corner was not a safety. The block game drew heavy criticism from all quarters, many demanding a return to strict rugby rules.

The 1882 rules. The one-possession problem now caused an emergency meeting of the IFA. The league met in April of 1882 to consider the outcry against the block game. Before that, various groups had lobbied Walter Camp and others to return to the rugby game. However, Camp and the other representatives were convinced that they could remedy the problem and preserve the scrimmage. They could not agree on a solution at that April meeting, but at the regular meeting in October a new rule was proposed by Camp, the "five yard" rule, also called the "downs" rule. This may or may not have been Camp's original idea, since something like it had been proposed in the press during the furor over the block game.

Whatever its origin, the IFA decision-makers passed a rule that would solve the problem and take American football even further from its rugby ancestry. The rule stated: *If on three consecutive fairs and downs a team shall not have advanced the ball five yards or lost ten, they must give up the ball to the other side at the spot where the fourth down was made. Consecutive means without leaving the hands of the side holding it.* A "fair" simply meant putting the ball in play from out of bounds (another down). Why losing ten yards (later 20 yards) should earn a new first down remains somewhat of a mystery. In limited circumstances it might be preferable to lose ground but keep possession of the ball – such as when time is running out. But generally the rule made little sense, and it was discarded in a few years. The new five yard, three down rule not only proved to be the solution to the one-possession problem, but, along with the scrimmage rule, it established the basic architecture for the new American football game. It also brought about the marking of the field of play into five yard segments with white lines to assist the referee in determining if a first down were made or not. The gridiron was born.

The downs rule was primarily a correction of the unexpected effect of the scrimmage rule. However, it also had some implications for further development of the game. It gave a specific number of yards to be advanced in order to retain possession. Captains could now calculate with greater precision what type of plays would accomplish the first down. For instance, with second down and one yard to go, a strong power play into the line would be called for; or, with second down and six or seven yards to go, an end run or some kind of deception would be the appropriate call.

Was the downs rule the right choice? If the downs rule had not been adopted to prevent the one-possession problem, downing the ball in the touch-in-goal would have to be made a safety, and teams that could not get possession of the ball would have to rely on the safety for scoring. This solution to the one-possession problem does seem quite unsatisfactory, but alternatives may have been available. For instance, each team might be given seven or eight downs in which to score. Such a rule would have the advantage of not requiring measurement for first downs or gridiron lines on the field. A solution very much like this was adopted in later years in English Rugby League football. Another alternative would be to penalize the team in possession by giving a point to the opponents for each down in excess of seven, eight, or whatever number was appropriate. Other variations seem possible.

Play and rules 1883. Play in 1883 continued to spread among colleges and clubs throughout the country. Innovative formations and plays were invented, and the game seemed now to be well established. However, the scoring system remained a headache. The IFA addressed this problem at their October 1883 meeting and adopted a system that has remained in effect ever since. They decided to allocate points to each type of scoring. The new rule, urged by Walter Camp (who else?), provided: goals from the field counted as 5 points, safeties 1 point, touchdowns 2 points, and a goal after touchdown 4 points.

At a later meeting in December of that year the numbers were changed to: touchdown counted as 4 points, safety 2, goal after touchdown 2, goal from the field 5. This is the same system we have today, although the numerical values for each type of score have changed over time. The changes subsequent to 1883 were as follows: 1897 touchdown 6, touchdown failing goal 5, field goal 5, safety 2: 1904 field goal 4: 1908 forfeited game 1 – 0: 1909 field goal 3: 1912 touchdown 6, extra point 1: 1958 two point conversion possible: 1988 two points for touchdown scored from a fumble, interception, or blocked kick of an opponent's PAT.

Protective equipment. Protective equipment began to become more prominent in the 1880s and 1890s. Shin-guards were occasionally used back in the days of Association football. The nose guard is probably the next oldest device, dating back to the 1870s. It was usually constructed of rubber. Protection from slipping came in the early 1880s with shoes constructed with leather spikes or strips on the soles. Canvas jackets, although of dubious value as a protective garment, first appeared at Princeton in 1877, and canvas pants appeared shortly thereafter. In 1888 some teams began to replace the canvas with "moleskin," a heavy cotton fabric that accommodated internal pads better than canvas.

The reason that there is not a specific date for most of these devices is that wearing one was an individual decision of each player. There was, of course, a desire to protect oneself, but then there was a countervailing psychological need to be macho and avoid any wimpy things like pads. The first use of head protection came in 1886 when some players at a Princeton-Lafayette game used what was called a "head harness." Headgear advanced in popularity and technological design throughout the 1890s and beyond, although everything was leather at this time. Soft pads in the football pants and shirts (thigh, knee, shoulder pads) were gradually replaced by leather or more substantial materials.

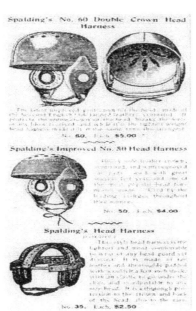
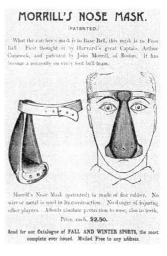

CHAPTER 6

DOWN THE WRONG PATH – POWER PLAY

1884 to 1894

Rough and Tumble. The development of the game in the 1880s gradually revealed a greater and greater use of force and power, a movement that reached its height in the 1890s. A reporter, describing a scrimmage in the 1884 Princeton-Yale game, said there was "real fighting, savage blows that drew blood, and falls that seemed as if they must crack all the bones and drive life from those who sustained them. . . . All the maddened giants of both teams were in it, and they lay there heaped, choking, kicking, gouging and howling." The public began to criticize the violence, and the value of big, strong, beefy players began to be more and more appreciated.

The Princeton V Trick. The beginnings of a new type of power play can be found in a device used by the Princeton team in 1884 known as the "V trick." This was the forerunner of many varieties of wedge formations. The V was first used on a kick-off, but it was also used later as a play from scrimmage. The players formed a V with the center (snap-back) at the apex. He was the only player on the kick-off line (center of field). The ball was put in play by giving the ball an "inch kick" then tossing it back to the quarterback who was in the center of the V. All the other players moved in lock-step forward to crash through the opposing line with the runner protected inside the wedge. The quarterback could run with the ball since this was not a scrimmage. The fullback ran behind the quarterback to push him when resistance was met. On a scrimmage the same formation was used.

The center snapped the ball to the quarterback who gave it to the fullback and then ran interference along with the other players. The V trick was used again by Princeton in 1886, and by 1887 it was being copied by other teams in one form or another. It eventually became the standard kick-off play.

Preparing for the V Trick

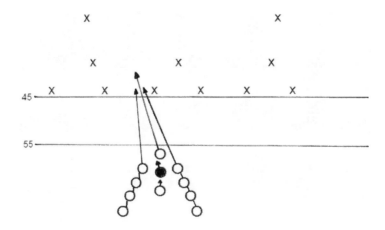

Diagram of V Trick on Kick-off

The IFA shaken up. In 1885 the Harvard administration and faculty decided to drop football. Their main objection was that the game had gotten out of hand, players fighting, rules ignored, and officials unable to control. This came as a blow to the IFA since the only other members were Yale and

Princeton – Columbia having withdrawn in 1884. But the group admitted Pennsylvania and Wesleyan in that same year, and the situation temporarily stabilized. Some observers speculated that the reason Harvard dropped out was that it feared playing Yale who had beaten the Crimson soundly in the previous two meetings. However, Harvard's complaints were not without merit. In that year the IFA enacted a rule making the maul-in-goal more difficult and dropping the judges from the roster of officials – an admission that they were nothing more than biased advocates. As they had in 1884, the rule-makers increased the penalties for offside infractions and unnecessary roughness.

Penalties. In the latter half of the 1880s the IFA became very concerned about violations of the rules and began to enact penalties to help with enforcement. The types of penalties varied and were changed from year to year. An official could disqualify players for certain kinds of conduct; he could award the ball to the other team for certain infractions; he could declare loss of down; he could penalize in yards, and he could even award points to the team not committing the foul. One of the infractions that drew the most attention was offside (see below). In spite of these attempts to put some bite in the rules, there remained only one official to enforce them, and this proved to be an impossible job. This was partially remedied in 1887 when an additional "umpire" was authorized.

Attendance. The practice of holding Thanksgiving Day games at large stadiums began in 1878 when the IFA championship was held at Hoboken, New Jersey. In 1880 the annual game was moved to the Polo Grounds (later called Manhattan Field) in New York City. This practice continued for two more decades. The 1882 block game brought a crowd of 10,000. The paid attendance increased to 23,000 in 1893 and up to 40,000 in 1895. This was important to the college teams because they lacked facilities that would accommodate large crowds, yet their operating revenue came mainly from paid attendance at games. For the same reason the Thanksgiving Day game, held in a large metropolitan stadium, became an annual event for the

University of Chicago, Georgetown University, the University of Missouri, and others.

Changes in 1886-87. Although the IFA had done practically nothing to meet Harvard's objections, that school again joined the league in 1886. In that year the league further standardized the ball. It was to be the Lillywhite No. J ball manufactured in England by the Lillywhite Company (the name has no connection to the color of the ball). There was no new ball size designated in '86, but a few years later, a Spalding athletic equipment company advertisement confirmed the 27-inch circumference as "regulation" size.

In 1887, besides adding the umpire, the IFA modified the rules to say that teams "must" try for goal after a touchdown as opposed to the previous wording that teams "shall" try for goal after a touchdown. This was intended to prevent teams from intentionally missing the goal to score another touchdown. Since the value of the touchdown in scoring had increased, teams who circumvented the rules were able to run up the score on teams with relatively weak defenses. In that same year a change was made in rule-making authority which eventually proved to have significant consequences. The IFA voted to establish an "Advisory Graduate Committee" to review rules and recommend changes to the parent organization. The remaining student rule-makers were being squeezed out. Walter Camp became one of the original committee members.

The offside problem. A player was offside, of course, whenever he was positioned between the ball and his opponent's goal. Blocking of an opponent by a player to help his teammate ball-carrier advance the ball was not permitted in rugby. This was not made a straightforward rule, but it was nevertheless strictly observed, and it was indirectly supported by the offside rules. However, when the Americans adopted the scrimmage rule, an unforeseen consequence occurred. As soon as the ball was snapped, the entire line was offside. According to Rule 23, being offside meant that the player "is out of the game and shall not . . . in any way interrupt or obstruct any player until he is again on side." Of course, the linemen in the American scrimmage were very busy interrupting and obstructing; it was called blocking. Amazingly, at the time apparently no one raised a question about the practice. The famous coach Amos Alonzo Stagg observed at a later date, "The original offside rule remained unchanged in the Rule Book until 1906, but it was honored only in the breach."

The problem aggravated. The offside problem of blocking in the line, although entirely ignored, was made worse by the increasing use of interference. As mentioned above, Princeton had introduced the practice of running interference for a ball carrier in the late rugby period. In theory at least, at that time the blockers did not run ahead of the runner. But this restraint did not last. The most brazen violation of the offside rules came about with the V trick. The ball carrier was concealed and protected by interferers running ahead of him. No objection was made by anyone. Again as Stagg put it, "This entering wedge having been accepted by common consent, Princeton in 1884 sent its interference boldly ahead of the ball, and opposition again copied instead of challenging." He added, "Interference was a direct and categorical violation of this offside rule."

A big dilemma. If the offside rules had been enforced as written, the game would have changed drastically. Things had probably progressed way too far for this to happen, so it seems that the offside rules should have been repealed, or severely modified, especially if the rule-makers had reconsidered the whole question of offside. The offside rules required that both the linemen and the backs (except the snapback) line up behind the quarterback instead of on the line of scrimmage. It's possible that some kind of standard formation would evolve from this with plays to fit. The defense would probably gain an advantage in rushing because they could build up some momentum before contact with the offensive players. It seems likely that passing (lateraling) the ball among carriers would pick up, especially since running interferers in front of a ball carrier would be illegal. The game would be quite different from what it was. Why didn't the rule change that was obviously called for – modifying the offside rules – take place? Another mystery.

A "solution" produced? In 1888 a rule was adopted by the IFA in which "*the players in the rush line are prohibited from blocking with extended arms.*" Commenting on this rule later, coach John Heisman reminisced, "The legitimacy of this sly move [offside blocking] was tacitly recognized when a rule was adopted in 1888 that declared that blocking 'with extended arms' was prohibited, which implied that blocking with the body would be permitted." The 1888 rule was followed by a rule in 1889 that provided, "*The side which has the ball can interfere with the body only; the side which has not the ball can use hands and arms as heretofore.*" At least in retrospect these rules were regarded as a justification for the offside behavior even though the offside rules were not repealed. Although this was a rather implausible reading of the new rules, it was Walter Camp's view and was generally accepted. This interpretation meant that the only significant application of the offside rules would be to keep players on their own side at the commencement of a scrimmage and to prohibit the forward pass.

Changes in 1888-89. Besides the rules on blocking/interference, several other rules were enacted in 1888 and 1889. The maul-in-goal was finally eliminated. Officials were authorized to use whistles. More penalties were enacted, and tackling was permitted between the hips and the knee. The latter rule made it easier to tackle and thus gave the defense an advantage. Previously the prohibition against tripping had been interpreted to prevent tripping by using hands and arms, thus making tackling below the hips illegal. The offenses tried to compensate with more blocking by moving the linemen closer together and also moving linemen into the backfield with new blocking schemes. These developments rapidly led to "mass plays" and "momentum plays."

The turn to mass and momentum plays might be called the Napoleonic strategy. The accepted wisdom in military circles, dating at least from Napoleon's time, was that the enemy line should be attacked with a superior number of troops who could break through and then harass the enemy from the rear. The breakthrough had to be done quickly to prevent the enemy from moving more of its own troops to the battle site. There are a number of indications that "advisors" (coaches) to the football teams were aware of this bit of militaria. In fact, Harvard coach Lorin F. Deland, inventor of the flying wedge (see below), was known as an expert on military maneuvers.

Mass plays. The legitimation of interference no doubt accelerated the invention of various types of mass play. It was probably even more important than the rule permitting tackling below the waist. The idea of a mass play, the Napoleonic strategy, was to assemble blockers (or interferers) around the ball carrier so as to strike at one point in the defensive line. Those interferers ahead of the runner would block the opposition, and the interferers behind the runner would push and boost him forward. These mass plays were relatively slow in developing, so the defensive players had an opportunity to move to the point of impact. This meant both sides contributed to a large pile of players at that site. This made the pushers' job important. They could propel the runner forward and move the whole pile, or they could lift the runner and shove him over the pile.

Mass on the defensive tackle.

The pulling guard. One of the first efforts to enlist linemen in the role of interferer was the pulling guard. Instead of blocking straight ahead as usual, the guard would pull back from his position, turn, and run toward one side or the other to block opponents in an off-tackle or end run play. Yale used this innovation in 1889, and it was picked up by others later. The invention is usually attributed to Walter Camp who at that time was an "adviser" to the Yale team. Yale's success with the pulling guard was largely due to all-American Walter "Pudge" Heffelfinger. He was an amazing player who could be counted on to mow down opposing tacklers and clear the way for the ball carrier.

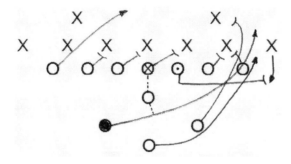

The Pulling Guard. Left Half off tackle. Guard blocks defensive end.

The ends back formation. The next step in the evolution of mass plays was the "ends back" formation invented in 1890 by Amos Alonzo Stagg as a player-coach for the Springfield (Massachusetts) YMCA team. In this scheme the ends played back behind the line of scrimmage about two yards. This change of position allowed them to run interference around end, off tackle, and even into the center of the line. In some plays they carried the ball, always, of course, after a hand-off from the quarterback. This formation was versatile, and Stagg diagrammed some 40 plays using it in his 1893 book (written with Henry L. Williams) entitled *A Scientific and Practical Treatise on American Football for Schools and Colleges.*

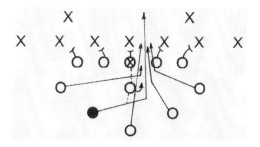

Ends Back Formation. Left halfback carries between center and guard. Fullback, right half and right end precede the runner through the hole, left end and QB push

Tackles back, guards back. There is some dispute as to who gets credit for the next development in mass play. The tackle back formation may have been Stagg's brain child, or it may have been devised by coach Henry Williams of Minnesota; some think Walter Camp also had a hand in it. The guards back formation is usually attributed to coach George Woodruff of the University of Pennsylvania. These new innovations appeared in the period 1891 to 1894. As with the ends back formation, two linemen were dropped back from the line into the backfield. This put them in a better position to run interference, allowing as many as five or six players to converge at a point in the defensive line to block for and push the ball carrier.

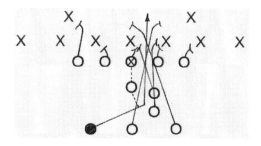

Guards Back Formation. Left half runs between center and tackle. Guards, right halfback, and fullback precede the runner. Quarterback pushes.

Revolving plays. One other type of mass play was a variation on the wedge. A wedge would normally move forward toward some point on the defensive line, usually between center and guard, or guard and tackle. One variation, invented by Stagg in 1891, was called the turtle-back. Players would line up, not in the usual V, but in an oval formation around the quarterback and the fullback. The center was the only player on the line of scrimmage. When the ball was snapped, the oval wedge would move forward as usual, but at a certain point, after two or three seconds, the players would change direction and pivot around the center. The quarterback would hand off to the fullback and then run interference. The play depended upon the defense quickly coming up to stop the usual wedge and then being caught in the wrong position. Princeton devised a similar play in 1896 called the revolving tandem. Players lined up in the ends back formation but then jumped into an oval formation when the ball was snapped. The entire formation then pivoted in one direction. Both of these plays had considerable success.

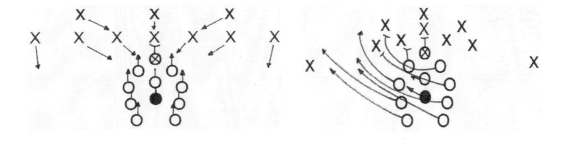

Revolving Wedge first step. Ball is snapped. Wedge moves forward. Defense converges.

Revolving Wedge second step. Wedge pivots and rushes left turning around center.

Revolving Tandem

Momentum plays. The mass plays discussed above pitting a large number of blockers against an equally large number of tacklers were exercises in brute force. Injuries were frequent and often serious. However, the most brutal invention was the momentum play. Imagine a group of three, four, or even five blockers and pushers running together toward a point in the defensive line *before* the ball was snapped. As they reach their target, the ball is snapped, and the runner follows the interference. The momentum of these players already in motion increases the force and violence of the contact with defenders. The momentum plays were in form like the mass plays discussed above; they might be wedge plays, or guards back, or tackles back, but the difference was that the interference was well in motion before the ball was snapped.

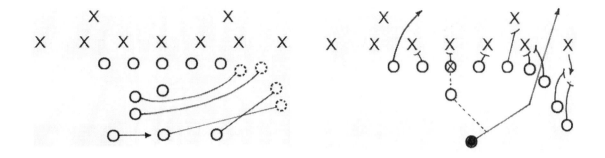

Guards back formation. Momentum play off tackle. Step 2. Ball is snapped. Guards, fullback and
Step 1. All backs except QB move toward hole.   right half run interference. QB pushes.

The Harvard flying wedge. The most famous momentum play was the flying wedge devised by Harvard coach Lorin F. Deland in 1892. It was only used on the kick-off. Since the opposing team was required to stand a minimum of 10 yards in front of the kicker, this gave the blockers even more time to build up momentum. The kicking team was divided into two groups standing about 25 yards behind the center of the field and thirty-some yards apart. The quarterback and fullback stood in between the two groups by themselves. At a signal the two groups rushed toward the target point to the left (or right) of the quarterback. As the groups met, one made a left turn, and the other continued on its path thus making a wedge. When they met at the kick-off line, the ball was inch-kicked by the quarterback and passed to the right halfback. The quarterback joined the interference. In the diagram below the play is run at the hole between the defensive right guard and tackle, but it could be run to either side and toward other targets. As with other successful innovations, the flying wedge was copied by other teams in subsequent years.

The flying wedge

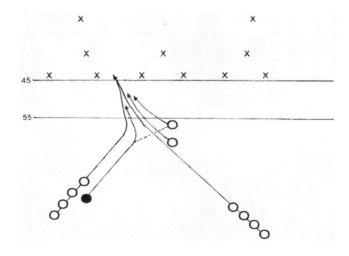

Diagram of the Harvard flying wedge.

Deception and quickness. Not all plays in this period were of the mass type. Use of deception, sweeps around end, and reverses were also employed. When the quarterback received the ball from center, he often turned with his back to the defense. From this position he could lateral, hand off, fake a hand-off or even fake two hand-offs. For a few seconds it was difficult for the opposing linemen to know who had the ball. This, of course, gave an advantage to the offense. Here are a couple of deception plays used by famous coaches Amos Alonzo Stagg and Fielding Yost in the '90s:

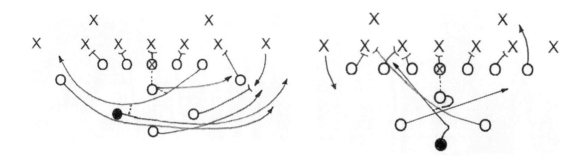

Stagg"s tackle criss-cross. Right tackle receives handoff from QB, then hands off to left HB going the other way. QB, FB, and RH run interference.

Yost's fake. QB fakes handoff to LH then hands off to fullback going between LG and LT. Right half runs interference. QB pushes.

The coach is defined. It is in the early 1890s that the institution of the coach becomes established. Prior to that time the captains and other experienced players did the coaching, although they occasionally had some guidance from former players. Coaching smacked of professionalism, frowned upon in most sports at this time. Some schools had developed a practice of asking the captain from the previous year's team to act as an adviser, without pay of course. Walter Camp's experience was not atypical. He was a captain for two of his six seasons, and then he continued to advise the Yale team for several years after. But he was successful in the clock-making business, and he never considered taking compensation for his coaching efforts. The first person actually to be called a football "coach" was Lucius N. Littauer at Harvard in 1881, although he was unpaid. After one year his duties were taken over by alumni captains until 1886.

Stagg sets the example. Amos Alonzo Stagg played at Yale for six years, graduating in 1888. He intended to become a minister and enrolled at the Springfield YMCA School, also called the Springfield Christian School or the International YMCA School. A part of the "muscular Christianity" movement, the mission of this school was to train its students to become athletic instructors who also spread the gospel. In Springfield Stagg organized a football team, played on it as an end, and coached it as well (see the "ends back" formation discussed above). While playing and coaching at Springfield in 1891, Stagg also served as coach for a secondary school, Williston Seminary, in neighboring Easthampton for a small sum.

William Harper, president of the University of Chicago and former Yale divinity professor, knew of Stagg's abilities. In 1882 Harper offered Stagg a job at Chicago for $2,500 per year as tenured head of the athletic department and football and baseball coach which he accepted. Stagg also played quarterback on his first Chicago team. With his remuneration at Williston and later at Chicago, Stagg is usually considered the first paid football coach; the fact that he was appointed as a regular faculty member (professor of physical culture), with tenure, further legitimized this position.

Like Camp, Stagg saw the attraction of football as the achievement of a cooperative enterprise. As he put it in 1893, "American football is pre-eminently a game for the practice and display of what is known as 'team play.' No other game can compare with it in this particular. . . . To get eleven men to use their individual strength, agility, and speed, their wit, judgment, and courage, first in individual capacity, then working with one or two companion players, then as eleven men working as one, is a magnificent feat in organization and generalship." Stagg diagramed 69 different plays in his 1893 book – published before the forward pass was authorized.

Coaching becomes respectable. Institutions playing football began to realize that an experienced coach meant a winning team. In the 1890s coaches who later became famous were finding paying positions at various schools. Glenn S. "Pop" Warner took a job at Georgia in 1895 for $35 per week.

John W. Heisman went to Oberlin in 1892 as a coach-player; he did not receive a salary, but would occasionally receive a "pass the hat" bonus after victories. He moved to Buchtel College (now University of Akron) the next year where he received a salary of $750 per year as head coach.

George W. Woodruff of "guards back" fame served as an unpaid coach for Penn while he attended law school there beginning in 1889 but was hired as crew and football coach of the Quakers for the annual sum of $1,300 in 1892.

Henry L. Williams, who played with Stagg and Heffelfinger at Yale, took a job teaching at Siglar Academy in Newburgh, New York, in 1891. He was asked to coach the Army team at nearby West Point. He probably was not paid for this service. In 1892 Williams entered the University of Pennsylvania School of Medicine. To help meet expenses he began coaching at Penn Charter School, a secondary school in Philadelphia. He also officiated at some of Penn's football games where he observed the tactics of George W. Woodruff. Upon completing medical school he served as a resident at Harvard hospital followed by two years as instructor in gynecology at the Penn medical school. He also spent time in Berlin and Vienna to further his medical study. In 1900, at the recommendation of Stagg, he accepted the first full time coaching job at Minnesota at a salary of $2,500, although he continued his medical practice while coaching.

A coach who produced a winning record could expect to move up. Fielding Yost began at Ohio Wesleyan in 1897, moved to Nebraska in 1898, then to Kansas in 1899, and on to Stanford and San Jose State in 1900, and finally to Michigan in 1901 where he received a salary of $2,000 plus living expenses.

All of these coaches, went on to much greater fame and fortune. However, in those days they would not be seen pacing the sidelines and yelling at players. Their work was at the drawing board and on the practice field. They were not allowed on the sidelines at games, and substitutes were not allowed to bring plays into the game.

CHAPTER 7

CRITICISM AND REACTION

1894 to 1896

An ugly game. The wedge, mass, and momentum plays that these ingenious coaches had devised under the rules of 1888 produced an ugly game. Ugly or not, those kinds of plays were winning games. And, the games were well attended. Crowds grew. Fans became enthusiastic. Some cheered for the slugging, kicking, punching, and gouging as well as the meritorious legitimate plays. It was becoming clear that the game's violence was one of its main attractions yet also its target of criticism. Two types of football observers began to emerge: those who loved it and supported it, and those who detested it and thought it should be abolished.

Publicity. The increasing popularity of football in the 1880s and early 1890s was revealed not only in attendance at big games, but in more comprehensive reporting in the mainstream press. This included, of course, reporting of injuries and deaths that occurred in the course of play. The public was made more aware of the dangers of the game, and an anti-football sentiment set in among some segments of the population. One of the most powerful voices opposing football was President Charles Eliot of Harvard. Eliot was in favor of abolishing the game, but he was never able to muster enough support at Harvard to get the job done. Nevertheless, he was a powerful and vocal critic. His criticism and that of others could not go unnoticed by the game's rule-makers.

The IFA fizzles out over eligibility problems. The IFA met in 1893 and discussed at length the problem of eligibility. This had been discussed during 1889, and the matter had generated some hard feelings. Players were supposed to be students at the institutions that fielded the teams. One of the problems was that some individuals, known as tramp players, moved from school to school simply to play football. It was known that incentives were given to these players, but nothing was proven at this time. Other players continued on past their undergraduate days by enrolling in graduate or professional schools at the same institution, thus lengthening their playing days from four years to five, six, or seven. Walter Camp himself had played almost six years at Yale as an undergraduate and as a medical student. Still other players enrolled in one or two courses, which they may or may not have attended, instead of becoming full time students.

In an effort to resolve this problem, at a meeting in January of 1893 Yale proposed the "undergraduate rule" limiting the eligibility of football players to undergraduates who were candidates for a degree. Wesleyan voted with Yale and Princeton to adopt the rule. Penn strongly opposed it. Then, at a meeting of the IFA in October of that year, Penn and Wesleyan withdrew from the league because of the undergraduate rule. This left Yale and Princeton, represented by Walter Camp and Alex Moffat, as the only remaining rules committee members and school representatives of the IFA.

Some new rule-makers. The pullout of Penn and Wesleyan hit the IFA at a particularly delicate time because pressure was mounting from various quarters either to abolish football or reform it. Some New York alumni and boosters of football at the big time schools were influential in getting the University Athletic Club of New York to invite representatives of Harvard, Penn, Princeton, and Yale to a meeting to take action to save football. Paul Dashiell, noted referee, was also asked to join. The group met in February and again in May of 1894 at the Athletic Club, calling themselves the "Intercollegiate Rules Committee" (IRC). Since this committee was only concerned with rules of the game, they were not bothered with the political problems of player eligibility, scheduling of matches, or awarding championships. They were not forming a league. They elected the experienced Alex Moffat of Princeton as chairman and Walter Camp of Yale as secretary, and then proceeded to enact eight new rules mainly designed to reduce the violence of the game.

Rules of 1894. The most important of the rules enacted by the IRC were: *a linesman was added to the referee and umpire as an official, dividing up the duties and presumably making enforcement of the rules more efficient; a player making a fair catch was required to hold up his hand as a signal with penalties for tacklers who ignored the signal; the length of the game was reduced from 90 to 70 minutes and divided into two halves, to avoid fatigue; piling on was penalized; kick-offs and kick-outs were required to go at least ten yards, thus eliminating inch-kicking and the use of momentum plays on kicks (including the V trick and the flying wedge); and no more than three men on offense were allowed to move before the snap, thus limiting but not eliminating momentum plays from scrimmage.* Viewed together, these rules could be expected to reduce the roughness of the game, but they seemed to critics to be a partial and weak response to the problem.

Facts and figures. Harvard's board of overseers was torn between boosters of football and opposition to the sport by President Eliot and many faculty. In 1894 they decided to conduct a study to determine the true extent of the injury problem. They asked Walter Camp to conduct the study! Camp did a brilliant job. He did a survey of players, former players, faculty associated with football, and prep school administrators. He published the results of the survey along with several essays by persons favorable to the game (including Walter Camp) as a book entitled *Football Facts and Figures*. Camp may not have included some of the negative reports that he received, but the book was a stunning propaganda success. The report concluded that injuries due to football had been greatly exaggerated by the press and that in fact football was actually safer than several other sports.

A bad year for football. The games in 1894 among the former IFA members proved to be disasters. Yale beat Harvard 12-4 in what was called the "Hampden Park Blood Bath." Four players were seriously injured on each team. Because of this, neither team would play the other in the ensuing three years. Pennsylvania beat Princeton 12-0 with the game ending in a brawl. As a consequence, they severed football relations for 40 years. The quarterback for Georgetown University in Washington, D.C., was killed when targeted by players of the opposing team who broke his neck. Georgetown immediately dropped football. The powers that be restricted teams at Army, Navy, and Cornell to playing games only at home. So, in spite of Camp's happy survey and the new IRC "reform" rules, the sport's reputation did not improve much in this grim year.

Direct pass from center. In 1895 the Yale team began using a direct pass from the center to the fullback. This allowed the fullback to punt the ball more quickly than before by eliminating the lateral pass from the quarterback. The rules still prohibited the fullback, as the first player to receive the snapback, from running forward. Arguably, the pass to the fullback did not satisfy the scrimmage rule which said that the player receiving the ball was designated the "quarterback." However, no one pressed this argument. The new practice was viewed suspiciously at first, but, as with most successful innovations, other teams soon imitated the practice. Apart from punting, it was a significant development because the limitation on running forward was dropped in 1903, thus permitting any back to receive the center snap and run forward.

Confusion in 1895. The pressure to de-brutalize the game increased. Camp and Moffat took it upon themselves to invite Harvard and Penn to another rule-making meeting in March of 1895. The main bone of contention was the continued use of mass and momentum plays. Yale and Princeton favored abolishing them, and Harvard and Penn wanted to keep them.

Several more meetings were held, but agreement could not be reached. In the fall Harvard and Penn, joined by Cornell, put out their own rule modifications that permitted the mass and momentum plays. Yale and Princeton also came up with their own set of modifications, severely limiting the mass and momentum type of play. These two sets of rules, together with the rules as modified in 1894, were published for the benefit of the football world. Now a team could choose to play by any of three sets of rules – provided it could get its opponent to agree to one of them.

The situation was displeasing to say the least, especially among smaller schools and schools in other parts of the country who were used to following the leadership of the big eastern universities. In the mid-west President James Smart of Purdue called a conference to address the situation. Purdue invited Chicago, Illinois, Lake Forest, Northwestern, and Wisconsin. They met in Chicago, calling themselves the "Intercollegiate Conference of Faculty Representatives," eventually to become known as the Big Ten. They affirmed the principle of faculty control of athletics, agreed upon rules of eligibility, and forbade players to accept gifts or pay. They would meet the following year and thereafter with Michigan replacing Lake Forest and Minnesota added. Other associations were also being formed around the country.

1896 -- Rescuing the rules. The handwriting was on the wall. The big eastern universities could see that their authority as football leaders and rule-makers would soon be challenged unless they did something to rectify the rules situation. The two eastern factions met in March of 1896, and agreed to merge the two committees. Represented were Cornell (L. M. Dennis), Harvard (J. H. Sears), Lehigh and later Navy (Paul Dashiell), Pennsylvania (John C. Bell), Princeton (Alexander Moffat), and Yale (Walter Camp). Continuing to act as the IRC, but generally just called the "rules committee," the group invited suggestions for rule changes from a large number of colleges throughout the country.

They got a good response, and they adopted five new rules which they thought would quiet critics. The most significant rule dealt with mass and momentum plays. It provided that *no offensive back "shall take more than one step toward his opponent's goal before the ball is in play without coming to a full stop."* It further required that *at least five players must be on the line of scrimmage when the ball is snapped. If six players are in the backfield, then two of them must be outside the ends or at least five yards behind the line.* Because of the required positioning of the players in the backfield, these rules eliminated wedge plays, guards-back plays, and tackles-back plays. The limitation on movement slowed down the momentum plays. Ingenious as coaches were, they soon learned to circumvent these rules in spirit if not literally.

Authority accepted. Surprisingly, the authority of this rules committee was immediately, if reluctantly, accepted. Other football conferences and leagues around the country continued to function, but their primary concerns at this point were the problems of eligibility, professionalism, subsidies to players, and faculty control of athletics. They mainly left the rules of the game as played to the traditional committee. The exact same individuals named above served without change as the rules committee for the next six years. From today's standpoint it seems incredible that these six gentlemen could exercise the power that they did.

The rules were published every year in Spalding's Official Football Guide edited by Walter Camp. When the IFA was functioning (pre-1894), the official rules were attributed in these publications to the rules committee of the American Intercollegiate Football Association (IFA) which had been formed by agreement and even had a written constitution. After that, for a couple of years, they were attributed simply to "The Rules Committee." Then, until the big change in 1905-06, they were attributed to the "Rules Committee as recommended to the University Athletic Club." Of course, the

University Athletic Club (of New York) never had any authority to do anything, including approving rules!

CHAPTER 8

CALM BEFORE THE STORM

1896 to 1905

A festering problem. The years between 1896 and 1903 did not see much innovation in rules, and most of the formations and plays were carry-overs from earlier years. Of course, the mass plays were less extreme because of the rules modifications of 1896, and the momentum plays had been substantially restrained. However, it was still possible to put six men in the backfield and concentrate interference on a spot in the defensive line. So, battering-ram football continued. And so did football injuries.

More and more people were joining in to the opposition to football including some of the press. Teams and leagues outside the northeast also felt discontent, and by 1901 they had begun to modify the rules of play for their own conferences. One rule, enacted by the IRC committee in 1900, provided, *"There shall be no coaching either by substitutes or any other person not participating in the game."* This expanded the prohibition of coaching on the sideline just slightly, probably indicating that this rule was being violated in practice.

Cheerleading. While the coaches were not permitted on the field, cheerleaders were. In 1898 one Johnny Campbell took megaphone in hand

and proceeded to lead cheers for the Minnesota Golden Gophers. Rehearsed cheers by fans in the stands had been around for years, but Campbell's on-the-field lead was a first. Other schools imitated the Minnesota exploit, and soon there were male cheerleaders at many football games. Women cheerleaders did not appear until 1923, again at Minnesota.

New plays. A few new playing innovations were introduced in this period. The tackle-back (singular) and the trap (also called mouse trap) were introduced at Yale in 1900. The tackle-back was Henry L. Williams, idea who passed it on to Walter Camp. This was a way of arranging the backfield so that a modified mass play could still be executed under the new rules of 1896. One halfback was placed parallel to the quarterback and outside the end, and a tackle was brought back into the backfield. The fullback had to be five yards behind the line of scrimmage. Many different plays could be run from this formation, the advantage being that the extra back (the tackle) was available to run interference. This differed from George Woodruff's guards-back formation in that two of the "extra" backs had to be located either outside the ends or five yards deep.

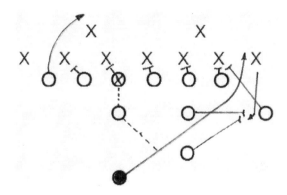

Tackle-back formation with fullback running off tackle.

The trap was not a formation or a play, but a blocking technique. Camp realized that defensive linemen were charging forward vigorously, and that their momentum might be used against them. He came up with the idea of allowing one defensive lineman to charge unopposed into the backfield a small distance and then to be blocked from the side by a backfield player. By vacating the place in the line where he normally would be challenging a blocker, the trapped player left a hole through which the ball carrier could penetrate the line. Yale alone was successful in using this technique for several years, and it later spread. Its use continues today.

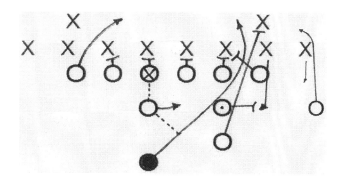

Trap from tackle-back formation. Defensive lineman charges past line of scrimmage. Backfield tackle blocks. Fullback carries.

At Northwestern University in 1900 coach C. M. Hollister established a new formation called the "Northwestern Tandem." This was the first "I" formation in football. What made it different from other formations designed to promote maximum interference for the ball carrier was that it could effectively be turned to either right or left. The defense could therefore not shift to counteract the tandem blocking before the snap as it could with other formations that weighted the backfield to one side or the other. Northwestern used this formation successfully, and it was imitated by other teams.

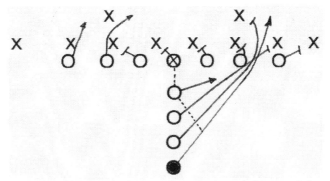

The Northwestern Tandem being used against an eight man defensive line.

Halfbacks precede the fullback carrying the ball, and quarterback pushes.

Defensive moves. Defenses were generally shifting from seven man lines to eight or nine man lines to counteract the mass plays. The three-point or four-point stance was also being endorsed by some coaches and accepted by linemen at this time. Common defensive formations were: the seven box, the seven diamond, the seven-three-one, the eight-two-one, and the nine-one. The "one" was the fullback (now safety) who played quite some distance back of the line of scrimmage; his job was to field punts. All other players were programmed to seek out and tackle the ball carrier or to disrupt the interference. Some coaches had the center line up on the line then retreat back quickly before the ball was snapped to a linebacker position (called "rush-line-back" at this time). A linebacker would often push the lineman in front of him to give him momentum. If the offensive backfield was unbalanced, the defensive line would shift as soon as possible to compensate. The play of the ends and the backs would vary depending upon the kind of play by the offense that was expected. Here are illustrations of the two approaches:

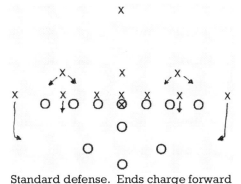 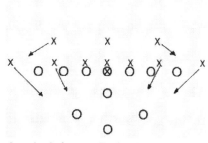

Standard defense. Ends charge forward and force play to the inside.

Pennsylvania defense. Ends charge inward to disrupt interference. Linebackers cover outside.

Everything's fine: the Dexter Report. While the rules committee had made some efforts to tame the game in 1896, not much had been done since then, and criticism of its violence from various quarters continued. A new defense of the game came in 1902. Like Camp's survey and report of 1894, the results of a new investigation seemed to show that the violence had been greatly exaggerated. Professor Edwin G. Dexter of the University of Illinois made a study of injuries and fatalities over a ten year period. His findings were based on a survey of presidents of some sixty colleges and universities. His data showed that more than 22,000 students had participated in football over the ten-year period. Only three deaths and eight permanent injuries were reported, and two of the deaths were not directly caused by the football injury. Dexter pointed out that newspaper stories of injuries had often been distorted and magnified. Although critics found flaws in Dexter's study, it did offer solid evidence that the injury problem may have been overblown. The report was published in Spalding's Official Guide for 1903 along with the usual rule changes and other information.

Football, yes. In spite of President Eliot's enmity toward football and a rising chorus of critics, Harvard's overseers decided to build the first reinforced concrete football stadium on its campus in 1903. The structure was built to hold a crowd of 27,000 in permanent seats and 15,000 more in temporary bleachers. In the same year Franklin Field in Philadelphia, home of the University of Pennsylvania Quakers, was enlarged to accommodate 20,000. The long range financial benefits were substantial.

The 1903 Checkerboard. In 1903, feeling pressure from critics, the rules committee solicited suggestions from people interested in football for ways in which the game could be improved. There was a strong sentiment that the game be made more "open." In response the committee again made an effort to get away from mass tactics. Two new rules were important. First, the quarterback, or *whoever received the snap-back, was allowed to run with the ball and cross the line of scrimmage; however, he could not cross that line until he was five yards to the right or left of the point where the ball was snapped.* Presumably this would encourage plays around end rather than pounding up the middle. To aid officials and players in determining whether the ball carrier crossed the line of scrimmage outside the five yard limit, lines were drawn on the field at five yard intervals parallel to the sidelines. This produced a checkerboard effect. *The second rule required that seven men be on the line of scrimmage when the ball was snapped.* This, of course, limited the backfield to four and eliminated one or more of the interference runners in the mass plays.

Peculiarly, *these two rules applied only when the scrimmage began between the 25 yard lines.* Between the 25 yard lines and the goal lines, the old rules were in effect. So, the checkerboard existed only in the middle of the field between the 25 yard lines, and the rest of the field remained in the usual gridiron configuration. This was the first and only time that two sets of rules were put into effect for a single game, depending upon the teams' field position. It may have been regarded as an experiment by the committee.

The checkerboard.

A step forward, a step back. In 1904 the rules were changed again. This time the rule allowing the player receiving the snap-back to run with the ball across the line of scrimmage was extended to the entire field. The five yard requirement on either side of the point of snap-back was kept. This meant that the entire field became a checkerboard. The rule requiring seven men on the line, however, was not extended. Instead, a new rule requiring six men on the line was applied to the whole field.

It was also in this year that the IRC committee, at Walter Camp's suggestion, invited Amos Alonzo Stagg, the well-known Chicago coach, to join the committee. This was the first time that anyone from outside the elite eastern schools had served on the committee, and it was done to counteract objections from the Big Ten and other leagues that they were unrepresented.

CHAPTER 9

ABOLISH OR REFORM?

1905 to 1910

Pressure mounts. The anti-football forces had not disappeared in spite of the Dexter report in 1902. The problems of tramp players and professionalism continued to surface, and the game's serious injuries were given a big play by some newspapers. Then in 1905 several things happened that gave the abolitionists hope that the game could be eradicated.

First, several incidents occurred on the field that put football in an ugly light. In a game played between Penn and Swarthmore early in the season the Penn offense repeatedly aimed its mass plays at Swarthmore tackle Robert Maxwell. The battered Maxwell finished the game, but his smashed and bloodied face was photographed and widely circulated by the press. In the Columbia-Wesleyan game a Wesleyan player kicked a Columbia player in the stomach as he lay on the ground. The action was seen by everyone, and players and crowd charged onto the field. The riot was finally put down by police. In the Harvard-Yale game Harvard player Francis Burr attempted a fair catch of a punt, but two Yale players ignored the fair catch and ran into him. One, Jim Quill, struck Burr in the face, breaking his nose, and the other delivered a body blow that knocked Burr out. Paul Dashiell, perennial rules committee member, was the referee, and he refused to call a penalty on Yale.

The Harvard-Penn game was no picnic, either. Two players were ejected and 210 yards of penalties were imposed. Finally, in a game between New York University and Union College on November 25 Union lineman Harold Moore attempted to tackle the ball carrier on a mass play and was knocked unconscious. Although he was quickly taken to the hospital, Moore died of a cerebral hemorrhage.

At the end of the season major press outlets published statistics for 1905 that showed 18 deaths and 149 serious injuries had occurred at all levels of play, and 3 deaths and 18 injuries had occurred at the college level.

Roosevelt intervenes. In October of 1905 the President of the United States, Theodore Roosevelt, entered into the great football debate. Roosevelt (a Harvard alumnus) invited representatives from Harvard, Yale, and Princeton -- the big three of football -- to lunch at the White House to discuss problems of the game. The president invited Walter Camp and "another man from Yale," Harvard's William T. Reid (coach) and Edwin H. Nichols (team physician), and Princeton's John B. Fine (rules committee member) and Arthur T. Hildebrand (coach). Camp brought John E. Owsley (coach) as the other Yale representative. Roosevelt was not an abolitionist; he was a strong supporter of the game. But he expressed concern about a number of things, especially cheating and crooked play. A wide-ranging discussion followed for about two hours.

When the meeting concluded, the president asked the representatives to issue a joint statement about their intentions. This statement was drafted on the train ride home, and Camp submitted it to Roosevelt by mail for review. Roosevelt approved it a day or two later, and it was released to the press. The statement pledged, "to carry out in letter and spirit the rules of the game of football relating to roughness, holding, and foul play." The statement itself was innocuous and contained no specifics; it did not even suggest that rules changes might be made. However, the fact that the president used his influence to further the football debate was of great significance. It magnified the importance of the debate in the minds of the public and the press.

Some schools quit. Complete abolition of the game was a real possibility. After the unfortunate incident in the NYU-Union game both schools dropped football. Trinity and Duke followed suit. The Big Ten held a series of meetings in late 1905 and early 1906 to seriously consider abolition of the game. Wisconsin and Chicago faculty members were strongly in favor of dropping the game. Only student and alumni pressure pushed them to take a wait-and-see attitude. Northwestern did drop the game. The league voted to continue the sport only on condition that certain reforms were adopted. On the west coast a somewhat similar scenario developed with a different outcome. Stanford University and the University of California (Berkeley) were the principal big time teams in that area of the country. The presidents of both institutions wanted to discontinue football because of its brutality. In November of 1905 they agreed to drop the sport. In February of 1906 they agreed to substitute rugby in its place using the Rugby Union rules of 1871. They continued with rugby for the next ten years.

Assembling to meet the crisis. The rules committee met in December of 1905. They discussed possible changes in response to the situation, but they took no action. Slightly earlier, immediately following the NYU-Union tragedy, NYU chancellor Henry M. McCracken fired off a letter to Harvard President Charles W. Eliot asking him to lead a movement of college officials and faculty to address the football problem. Harvard's prestige as an academic institution and its history as a leader in the development of big time football would obviously lend great weight to such a movement. But Eliot, the old enemy of football, declined, indicating that football was not worth saving. He apparently did not realize that this was an opportunity to abolish the game.

Ignoring the rebuff, McCracken took it upon himself to invite nineteen colleges who had played NYU over the last ten years to a meeting in New York on December 8. Thirteen colleges attended. Harvard and Yale were not invited because NYU had not played them but also because Eliot was so negative about football and Yale's Walter Camp was viewed as part of the problem. Woodrow Wilson, president of Princeton, refused the invitation because, as he said, Princeton had its own set of reforms in mind. At the December 8 meeting several motions were made. The first one was to abolish the existing game. It failed eight to five. Football came that close to possible extinction. Voting in favor of the motion were Columbia, NYU, Rochester, Stevens Institute, and Union. Against were Fordham, Haverford, Lafayette, Rutgers, Swarthmore, Syracuse, Wesleyan, and Army. A second motion to reform the existing game passed. Realizing that the conference was not very representative, they agreed that other schools from around the country should be invited to the next meeting scheduled for December 24.

Abolition? We should consider what might have happened if the McCracken group had voted to abolish football. Realizing that the eastern schools had long been leaders in the game, their influence might have caused other schools across the country to drop the game as well, and American football would disappear. However, keep in mind that the really big boys, Harvard, Yale, and Princeton, were not a part of the McCracken group, and if they decided to retain football, they would also influence other schools. Although the Big Ten, the most advanced conference outside of the east, was considering abolishing the game, they ultimately decided not to do so. They might well have become the new rule-makers for the country if the McCracken vote had gone against football.

A new start. At the second meeting of the McCracken group sixty-eight schools were represented. The representation diminished with the distance from New York, but there were representatives from as far away as Texas, Colorado, Minnesota, and South Dakota. The group decided to form a permanent organization and called itself the Intercollegiate Athletic

Association of the United States (IAA). Its immediate task was to establish a committee to come up with new rules for the game that would accomplish necessary reforms. Major Palmer Pierce of West Point was elected president. Interestingly, a bit earlier, President Roosevelt had quietly impressed General Albert S. Mills, commandant of West Point, with the need to reform football.

Schools that were represented on the old committee (IRC) did not send representatives (Chicago, Cornell, Harvard, Penn, Princeton, Yale and Navy). As a first matter of business, the new organization had to face the problem of the existing rules committee (IRC). It was finally decided that a committee of the IAA would be appointed, and they would attempt to meet with the IRC jointly to propose reform rules. If the IRC was not receptive, the IAA committee would proceed on its own. An IAA committee of seven was appointed with Henry L. Williams, coach of Minnesota, as chairman, and meetings were scheduled by both committees for January 12 in New York.

Reid's ploy. Coach William T. Reid of Harvard was a recent member of the old rules committee (IRC) and one of the six who had met with President Roosevelt. He had maintained contact with Roosevelt indirectly because of the Harvard connection. A relatively young coach, Reid had come to favor serious rule modifications as a way to save the game. When he met with the old committee in December of 1905, he realized that no real reform was going to come from that group and that the old committee itself, especially Walter Camp, was going to be a significant stumbling block.

When McCracken issued his call, Reid saw his chance to advance reform. First, he stalled the old committee from taking any action by claiming that he was occupied in Cambridge trying to prevent the school from abolishing football. Whether the school's overseers were actually planning to do that is still an open question. In this effort Reid managed to have a letter published, addressed to the Harvard alumni athletic committee, in which he claimed that Harvard would drop football unless a series of reforms were enacted. These proposed reforms included, among others, ten yards for a first down (instead of five), the forward pass, and a neutral zone. Reid did have the blessing of the Harvard athletic committee on this, but they also instructed him to compromise. Of course, most interested parties recognized that if Harvard abolished football it would be a serious blow to the game.

Reid went to New York for the January 12 meeting, initially with the IRC committee, but instead, following instructions of the Harvard athletic committee, he quickly approached the IAA committee and asked to be recognized. A somewhat baffled committee agreed to hear Reid, and he presented the Harvard reform demands together with the threat that Harvard would drop football unless they were met. At this point the IAA did not have an agenda of specific reforms, so the Harvard demands were available to fill that need.

Changing of the guard. The IAA committee decided to admit Reid and went ahead and met with the old committee. The old committee was not overjoyed at the prospect of their power being diminished, but they recognized that there were no realistic alternatives. After considerable political wrangling, L. M. Dennis of Cornell who had served on the old committee was named chairman of the joint committee, and James Babbit of Haverford, serving and the new committee, was named secretary. In an apparently prearranged deal, Babbit immediately resigned and appointed William T. Reid to take his place. The significance of all this political maneuvering seems to be that Walter Camp had finally been squeezed out of the leadership. Camp was, however, retained as editor for publication of the rules.

The joint committee appointed four sub-committees to work on separate subjects and report back. The four areas of concern were:

eliminating brutality and foul play; creating a more open game; establishing a central list of approved officials; and the feasibility of testing proposed rule changes on the field. The four subcommittees met in five more sessions running from January to April. The new rules accepted by the full committee were published before mid-year. As a result, fans, players and coaches eagerly anticipated the upcoming 1906 season.

The 1906 rules. More new rules were enacted in 1906 than in any year since the adoption of the Rugby Union rules in 1876. One rule that was not adopted deserves some consideration. It was proposed, with variations, that the number of players in the defensive line be limited and that the position of the defensive backs also be regulated. Keep in mind that defensive arrangements at this time had included nine man lines with one linebacker in close position and occasionally even ten man lines. This proposal, combined with a rule requiring 10 yards for a first down, would presumably "open up" the game. It possibly could have been a real game-changer, but it died in subcommittee.

The most important rules that were ultimately enacted are as follows: *1. A forward pass is permitted, but with limitations – pass must be made by a back from behind the line of scrimmage; only ends and backs are eligible to receive; pass must be thrown and received five yards on either side of the center; a pass not touched by any player goes to the opponents at the spot where it touched the ground; an untouched pass that crosses the goal line is a touchback for the defenders; a pass that goes out of bounds goes to the opponents at the spot where it went out of bounds; the defense cannot throw a forward pass. 2. First down yardage is increased to 10 yards in three downs. 3. A neutral zone is created at the line of scrimmage equal to the length of the ball. 4. Time of game is shortened from seventy to sixty minutes with two halves. 5. Officials authorized include referee, two umpires, and a linesman.*

A number of other rules were also enacted that mostly dealt with penalties for holding, unnecessary roughness, and personal fouls. Another rule expanding the use of on-side kicks potentially could have opened up great possibilities, but it fizzled and was discarded a few years later. Walter Camp had been regarded by newer committee members as the reactionary who opposed reforms to the game. However, Camp had suggested several years earlier that a neutral zone be created, and, after observing some Canadian games, he also came around to favoring the ten yard rule for first down. And, he supported increased penalties for rough play. He continued to endorse these reforms in 1906. However, he was opposed to the forward pass.

Effect of the new rules. Except for the forward pass, the intended effect of the new rules was fairly clear. The neutral zone helped prevent the slapping and slugging that had been common along the line of scrimmage. It also gave officials a better chance to see such violations. Adding an additional official allowed greater control over the game and reduced roughness fouls. Reducing game time to sixty minutes with a ten minute halftime period presumably helped prevent fatigue. The ten-yard rule discouraged the bulldozer mass plays by making it more difficult to reach a first down using them. The mass play could usually be counted on to gain two or three yards, but now this would not be enough. So, it would be necessary to rely more on sweeps, reverses, deception, and the forward pass. The game would be "opened up." The Napoleonic strategy would have to be revised.

Sponsors of the forward pass certainly thought that it would "open up" the game. Various stakeholders had suggested in earlier years that it would open up the game. Coach John Heisman claimed that he had written Walter Camp on two occasions in past years asking the committee to consider it. Although the forward pass received the necessary eight votes on the committee to pass, not everyone was convinced that it was a good thing. Some thought it would completely change the sport into some kind of basketball game. Others thought that it would produce more rough play and injuries than it would prevent. Another view was that the forward pass was too big a step to take at one time because no one could really predict what its effect would be. Those holding this sentiment were no doubt influential in adding the various limitations that hedged in the passing rule.

The forward pass did, indeed, open up the game, although not immediately. It provided an opportunity for the design of a whole set of plays that would rival the ground game. And the combination of ground tactics combined with passes made great changes in both offense and defense necessary. New techniques in running pass patterns, pass blocking, throwing the ball, and faking passes and runs were just around the corner.

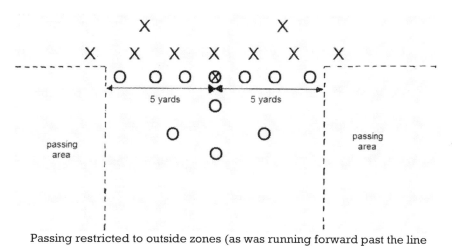

Passing restricted to outside zones (as was running forward past the line of scrimmage for the first receiver of the snap).

The new rules and the new committee that adopted them made one effect very clear: all interested parties realized that something was being done about the problems of football. Complaints had been listened to. New decision-makers more representative of the football world were at work. A serious attempt at reform had been made.

Passing not so easy. Passes in Association football, rugby, and American football, usually called "laterals," had always been done underhanded. Most passes were short and could be executed easily with two hands – a shovel pass. If a play called for a long lateral, an underhand swinging motion could be used with one hand and arm. This would work with sufficient accuracy up to twelve or fifteen yards. Sometimes the ball was thrown end over end and sometimes in a sort of lazy bobbing spiral. The shape of the ball did not help. In the old game there were never any intervening players between the passer and the receiver, so the pass could always be low. But now, a forward pass would usually have to be thrown high over the heads of intervening players and for substantial distances. What to do, and how to do it?

Amos Alonzo Stagg recalled that he had a player back in the 1890s that had developed a way of tossing the ball overhand at some distance with a spiral motion. He was a large man with big hands and a former baseball player. Stagg designed a play in which the movement went all to the right, but one player drifted off to the left. Then the thrower would stop and lateral the ball overhand, perhaps 25 or 30 yards, to the isolated player who then could run for a big gain. This was, however, quite atypical.

Most players had never seriously tried to throw the ball overhand. Various techniques were tried. The "flat hand" technique was mildly successful for passers who couldn't grip the ball. The ball was placed on the flat throwing hand, and then with a big wind-up the ball was heaved with a side-arm motion. Grasping the ball by the end and throwing it end-over-end would more or less work for short distances, but accuracy was not assured. Tossing the ball with two hands like a basketball pass across court was tried, but did not prove very satisfactory. The blimp like character of the ball made air resistance and wind real enemies of passing. The spiral overhand pass seemed to be the answer. It required the passer to grasp the ball toward one end with three or four fingers placed over the laces and then throw as in a baseball pitch with the fingers adding a spin. With the ball shaped like a watermelon this was not easy. For passers with small hands, it was practically impossible. Practice, practice, practice.

The flat hand pass   The underhand end-over-end pass

Receiving the ball had never been a problem with the laterals. However, with the forward pass, receivers had to learn to catch the ball with the hands, not the chest or body, and catching high passes or passes over the shoulder was something new too. Again, practice, practice, practice. Many coaches in 1906 felt that they did not have enough time to devote to practicing these new skills.

Passing catches on slowly. Most teams were reluctant to try the forward pass because of the drastic penalties that were incurred in case of a mishap. Loss of possession of the ball was something few coaches wanted to risk. The chances of making a gain were also small because of the forced passing on one end of the line of scrimmage or the other. Nevertheless, if a team was getting behind, or if time was running out, the pass was there as a last ditch opportunity to score or gain big yardage. This is how many teams used the pass. Other teams found that the occasional use of the pass helped open up the running game because defensive backs had to play back for a possible pass. It was a balancing of risks. With players unskilled at passing and receiving, the choice usually was to avoid passing. Occasional passing became the standard in the east, but mid-western teams were slightly more inclined to give the new play a try.

Eddie Cochems and St. Louis. Edward B. Cochems, who had played at Wisconsin, became the head coach at St. Louis University in 1906 after successful coaching jobs at several other schools. Influenced by John Heisman, Cochems was a believer in the forward pass. He knew, however, that considerable training and practice would be required to make the pass successful. St. Louis was a Catholic school, and Cochems was successful in getting permission to work out his team at a Jesuit retreat located on Lake Beulah in Wisconsin. In the summer of 1906 he took the team to Lake Beulah for two months where the players practiced morning and afternoon every day. Although the team worked on running plays and fundamentals, they also devoted considerable time both long and short passes. Cochems set up hoops so his passers could throw through them, and he devised a play in which the ball was lofted high and the receiver came to the designated spot to catch it while lineman interferers would collect around him. This was called the "Parabola Pass." Cochems' principal passer was a transfer from Wisconsin named Bradbury Robinson, a tall young man with large hands. He worked very hard on throwing a spiral pass and was eventually able to deliver the ball accurately over a 40 yard distance.

Eager to try out his new offense, Cochems was able to schedule a game with nearby Carroll College on September 5 in Waukesha, Wisconsin. In that game the first intercollegiate pass was thrown by Bradbury Robinson. It hit the ground without being touched, and St. Louis lost possession of the ball. However, Robinson succeeded with further passes, and St. Louis won the game 22 – 0. The team went on to post an 11 – 0 record including big victories over Kansas and Iowa, two highly respected teams. Cochems continued his success in 1907 and 1908, but then resigned under a cloud in 1909 after charges of professionalism (paying players, etc.) were made. His overall record at St. Louis was 25 wins, 5 losses, and 2 ties.

Experimenting with the pass. Other teams experimented with the forward pass in 1906 and the following years. Stagg at Chicago and "Pop" Warner then at the Carlisle Indian School in Pennsylvania both quickly developed pass plays for their game – even though Warner was opposed to the introduction of the forward pass. This aspect of the game continued to grow as passing skills improved among the players. In 1907 Stagg's Chicago completed 25 passes against Purdue, and Illinois completed 30 passes in a game against Northwestern. The pass received a boost from the rules committee in that year when a 15 yard penalty replaced the loss of possession in the case of an untouched incompletion. This, of course, substantially reduced the riskiness of passing. In that year Michigan coach Fielding Yost devised a famous "trick" play in a high profile game with Penn. The referee called the play illegal, so Penn won the game. However, as Yost diagrammed the play afterward for the press, it was apparently legal.

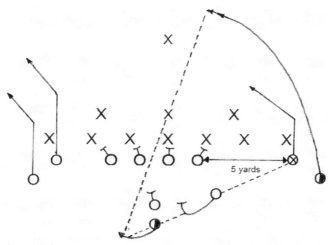

Yost pass play within passing area. Pass thrown and caught outside 5 yard limit.

As mentioned, other coaches, particularly Amos Alonzo Stagg and Glenn S. "Pop" Warner, were designing new pass plays and integrating them with the ground game. Here are a couple of plays from Stagg's 1906 playbook:

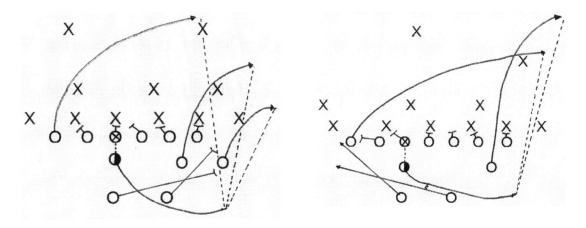

Quarterback sprint with option to pass or run.   Bootleg. QB fakes to halfback and passes.

In 1908 the passing game received a necessary adjustment with a new rule dealing with pass interference. It provided, *"While the ball is in the air for a forward pass, players of the defensive side may not use their hands or arms on opponents, except to push them out of the way in order to get the ball themselves. Players of the side making the pass, who are eligible to receive the pass, may use the hands and arms as in case of players going down the field under a kick. Neither side may, however, "hold" or "tackle" an opponent who has the ball."* This rule, of course, deals with a very difficult situation that presents serious problems for officials. It has been modified many times since 1908, but even today pass interference calls are often controversial.

The Minnesota shift. Another innovation in the period between 1906 and 1909 was the "Minnesota Shift" invented by coach Henry L. Williams. The rule changes of 1896 had pretty well outlawed momentum plays by prohibiting movement before the snap. Williams devised a way to achieve the effect of a momentum play while still staying within the letter of the law. His team would line up in a strange formation with several linemen in the backfield, then, on a signal, both the line and backfield would shift positions. As soon as they reached their new positions another signal would produce the snap-back, and the play would move into action. The second signal and the snap-back were so close to the movement that the players actually had some momentum going forward. The shift allowed the interferers and the ball carrier to gain an advantageous position before the defense had time to adjust. Williams' shift was the model and precursor of several other shifts used by various coaches and teams.

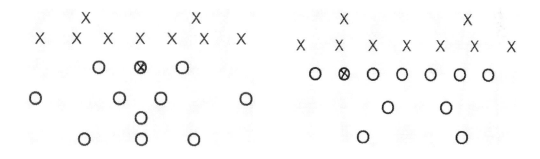

Minnesota shift: first position   Minnesota shift: position at snap

The single wing. The invention of the single wing formation by Glenn S. "Pop" Warner was the final important innovation in this period. Warner coached at several colleges, but his development of the single wing came when he was at the Carlisle Indian School in Pennsylvania. Warner's thinking was that the traditional or regular formation was a waste of time and manpower. This was the "T" formation in which the snap was to the quarterback who handed off or lateraled to another back. Warner reasoned that if the snap were made directly to the runner, the quarterback became available as another blocker, and the time between the snap and the reception in the runner's hands was shortened.

After experimenting with rearranging the backfield, Warner came up with a formation that was capable of deception, power plays, and forward passing. The formation was unbalanced in the backfield (to either side) and could be unbalanced in the line as well. Warner originally called it the "Z formation," and Walter Camp called it the "Carlisle formation." Later, Warner called the single wing the "A" formation and the double wing the "B" formation. The single wing was so effective that it was ultimately adopted by most of the teams in the country, replacing the old "regular" formation.

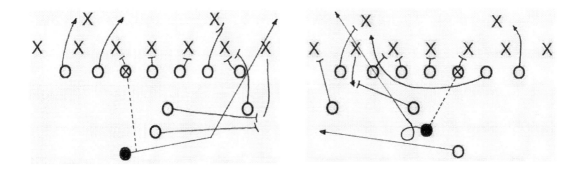

Single Wing right: tailback off tackle   Single Wing left: fullback spinner fake to tailback

The single wing offense usually used the fullback or the tailback as the runner or passer. The tailback in particular was in a position to run, pass, or kick. This gave rise in future years to the "triple threat" back who excelled at all three skills. Most of the famous players in the 1920s and 1930s were triple threats.

Marching band. To complete the innovations of this period it should be mentioned that the University of Illinois introduced the halftime marching band in 1907. This occurred during a game between Chicago and Illinois at Champaign. Although students at Rutgers had authored a song about football as early as 1876, the Illinois/Chicago contest also saw the introduction of the first football fight song to be used at games -- "Illinois Loyalty." As usual, these innovations were quickly copied by other schools.

CHAPTER 10

COMPLETING THE REVOLUTION

1910 to 1912

1909: a bad year. From 1906 through 1908 football had enjoyed a period relatively free from criticism. But 1909 brought the critics out again. Three serious events occurred in high profile intercollegiate games. A Navy cadet was paralyzed in a game with Villanova. An Army cadet died in that team's game with Harvard. Finally, a Virginia player was also killed in a game between Virginia and Georgetown. The newspapers had been keeping statistics since the ugly year of 1905. They suggested that the presumed safety provided by the rule reforms of 1906 was illusory.

Year	Deaths (college)	Injuries (college)
1905	3	88
1906	3	54
1907	2	51
1908	6	33
1909	10	38

Rule-makers go to work again. When the IAA committee met in 1910, Walter Camp still remained, but there were a number of personnel changes on the rules committee since 1906. This committee, still functioning as the "joint" or "amalgamated" committee, was generally sensitive to criticism and open to further reforms. Their authority was also bolstered by the fact that several major schools had joined the parent IAA since 1906, including Harvard, Chicago, Penn, and two thirds of the Big Ten schools. In 1910 the IAA changed its name to the National Collegiate Athletic Association (NCAA) and expanded its activities beyond rule-making. The rules committee again went to work with the specific objective of preventing injuries.

Rule changes of 1910. The major rule changes were very significant. *1. Seven men were required on the line of scrimmage at the snap. 2. Pushing and pulling the ball carrier by members of his own team, and interlocking hands and arms by interferers were prohibited. 3. The five yards to the sides of center limitation on both running the ball forward and in forward passing was dropped. (The checkerboard was history.) 4. Two more limitations were placed on the forward pass: the pass must be thrown from at least five yards behind the line of scrimmage, and it could be thrown no more than 20 yards past the line of scrimmage. 5. The game was divided into four quarters of 15 minutes each. 6. One back was allowed in motion before the snap, but he could not move forward toward the line of scrimmage.*

The requirement of seven men on the line and abolition of pushing and pulling finally meant that the old Napoleonic strategy could no longer be used. The mass play was dead. The new 20 yard limitation on the forward pass diminished its effectiveness, but this was shortly repealed. The value to the offense of the permitted man in motion was not immediately appreciated, probably because men in motion had always been used for momentum plays. But ingenious coaches in later years made good use of this device.

Play in 1910-11. Although there was pressure to make further changes in the rules in 1911, the committee decided to leave well enough alone and let the coaches and teams absorb the changes of the preceding year. To clean out the cobwebs, the rule-makers eliminated an old relic from rugby days: the center (snapper-back) could no longer kick the ball toward the opponent's goal to start a scrimmage. 1911 was also the year that intentional grounding of the ball first surfaced, at that time not regulated.

However, although the popularity of the forward pass under the new rules continued to grow, especially in the mid-west, south, and southwest, there remained opposition to this apparently successful device. At a rules committee meeting in 1911 a vote was taken to abolish the forward pass, and the vote passed! This vote was taken in the wee hours of the morning when several members of the committee were not present. Another vote was taken the next day, and the motion was barely defeated after southern and western members threatened to leave and form their own rules committee.

Could we do away with the pass? No. It seems clear with the benefit of hindsight that if the vote to abolish the forward pass had stuck, the game would have nevertheless gone on pretty much as it did. The committee, as it always had been, was heavily weighted with eastern school representatives, and the eastern schools were those least enamored of the forward pass. If they abolished it, the Big Ten and other conferences in the rest of the country would clearly have rejected this move, and they probably would have adopted their own set of rules in which the pass was accepted. This might well have led to a new national rules committee with more democratic representation, and the NCAA would become a regional organization, if it survived.

Big changes in 1912. The reforms of 1912 completed the shaping of the forward pass that had begun in 1906 and instituted other changes that made football recognizable as the same game played today. First, the dimensions of the field were altered to its present day size. *The length of the playing field was reduced from 110 yards to 100 yards. An end zone ten yards deep was created at each end of the field*; previously there was no recognized playing space behind the goal lines. Creation of the end zone was necessitated by changes in the forward pass rules. After considerable debate it was decided to leave the goalposts on the goal line. Second, *the kick-off was moved from midfield, formerly the 55 yard line, back to the forty yard line of the kicking team.* Finally, *a fourth down was added in which to advance 10 yards for a first down.*

Three important changes were made in the passing rules. First, *the 20 yard limit on passing beyond the line of scrimmage was removed.* Second, *a pass caught in the end zone was counted as a touchdown*; previously a pass caught behind the goal line would have been a touchback and possession given to the other team. Finally, and possibly the most important new rule, *the size of the ball was changed.* The "standard" size ball had been 27 inches in circumference in the small dimension. This was changed to 22 ½ to 23 inches, a reduction of 1.3 inches in the diameter of the center of the ball. Equally important, it also necessitated a smaller diameter toward the ends of the ball, making them more pointed. This allowed a passer with average size hands to throw a decent overhand spiral pass, and the ball no longer looked like a rugby blimp. Further reductions of one half inch in the small circumference were made in 1929 and 1934, and a significant change in the pressure inside the ball was made in 1930.

The Football

CHAPTER 11

REALIZING THE POTENTIAL OF THE NEW GAME

1912 to 1918

The Denison phenomenon. Denison College in Ohio was one of the first teams to utilize fully the new passing rules. In a scenario reminiscent of the Eddie Cochems episode at St. Louis, Denison developed a passing attack in 1912 that few teams could withstand. The offense was driven by George Roudebush, a tall player with large hands who could throw the ball long distances with great accuracy. The team compiled an impressive record in 1912 and repeated (with Roudebush) in 1913 and 1914, crushing most opponents. Playing in the Ohio Conference, Denison did not draw much attention from the eastern press, although its accomplishments were noted in the Chicago Tribune.

Notre Dame and publicity. For several years before 1913 Notre Dame had compiled an admirable record. However, this was a small mid-western school that did not play many major teams. Some Big Ten teams had even boycotted Notre Dame for allegedly playing "ringers." Searching for a chance to play a big-time opponent, new coach Jesse Harper, a Stagg protege, managed to schedule a game with Army in 1913. Army was one of the powerhouses of the eastern establishment. The Irish went east and stunned the cadets with a strong passing attack: score 35 – 13. Eastern fans could hardly believe that an unknown mid-western team could beat one of their best – and by passing too! Although this was hardly the beginning of the passing game, this feat gave great favorable publicity to two things – Notre Dame and the forward pass. Army learned from the experience and developed a passing attack of its own in subsequent games. Its victory over Navy in the same year may have had an equal value in publicizing the passing game in the east.

The beginning of bowls. The year 1914 saw the completion of the Yale Bowl, a stadium capable of accommodating 70,000 fans, much larger than anything that preceded it. Inspired by the Roman Coliseum, the oval arena served as the model for the later Los Angeles Coliseum, and the name eventually led to the use of the term "bowls" for post-season games. In that same year Princeton built Palmer Stadium capable of holding 40,000 spectators.

The Yale Bowl

Play in 1913-1917. There were a few minor rule changes in this period. One of the least significant rules was passed in 1913; snapping-back with the foot was outlawed. As we have seen, this was an ancient technique from the rugby scrummage and had not been used in decades. In 1914 intentional grounding was prohibited, and a pass out of bounds was simply declared a dead ball. Previously, such a pass resulted in loss of possession by the passing team. The kick-out after a touchback or safety, another old rugby antique, was eliminated, and the ball was required to be placed for a scrimmage. In 1916 a rule was enacted defining forward progress of a ball carrier and making that the point where the ball becomes dead. Previously, a ball carrier could be carried backward by defending tacklers, even across the goal line, and the ball became dead where he was downed (where the ball touched the ground).

The passing game progressed to become a staple of almost every team playing football. The important development at this time was to integrate the running and passing games. Stagg at Chicago and Warner at the Carlisle school had set the pattern. Fake passes made their appearance as well as fake running plays (play action passes). Eastern teams were coming around, and teams in the south and southwest were running up big yardage through passing. Oklahoma's undefeated team set passing records in 1915. However, as passing became common, teams were also improving in pass defense. Some figures from 1914 showed that interceptions outnumbered completions by two to one. Although he had opposed the forward pass from the beginning, Walter Camp had mellowed by 1916. He said, "[T]he game is beginning to crystallize along certain lines which provide for a fair equalization of attack and defense and produce a game that is interesting to players and spectators alike, and which offers an almost unlimited field for study of plans and tactics by the coaches." Here are a couple of innovative pass plays developed before World War I:

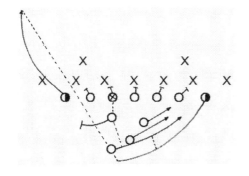 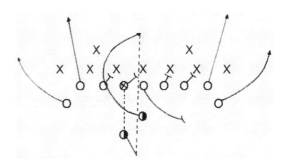

Play action pass play by Army coach Charles Daly. Tailback fakes run, end passes.

Pop Warner pass play using wide receivers as decoys. Run from the double wing formation.

The running game in this period also showed some innovations. The double wing was devised by Pop Warner. It was a more effective passing formation than the single wing. The punt formation had been used for a long time, but usually only for punting or a fake punt. Coach Stagg claimed later that he had used the punt formation in the 1890s for the running game. However, like a number of Stagg's claims made later in life, there seems to be no support for this, and other authorities have contradicted him on this point. If Stagg had had success with the punt formation as a running attack, it is likely that many other coaches would have imitated it immediately. However, many coaches did find it usable in the period after 1912 for both running and passing. The spread formation (or formations) had been tried occasionally as a surprise by coaches at Idaho, Arkansas, and perhaps others in earlier years, but it got regular use by coach Bob Zuppke of Illinois beginning in 1916. Although used for both runs and passes, this formation became popular with many teams who had outstanding passers, and in later years it was called "the run and shoot," "the shotgun," and the "air raid." As usual, all these new inventions were copied by many other teams.

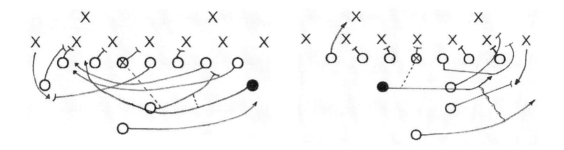

Double wing formation. Reverse to the short side.   Punt formation off tackle play. Runner has option to lateral to fullback. First option play. (Warner)

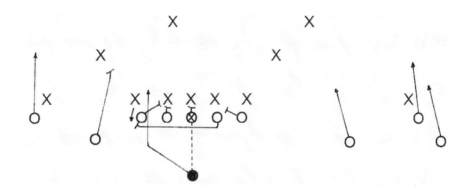

Typical spread formation. Run to left.

NCAA swallows IRC. By 1916 all of the schools that were represented on the old rules committee (IRC) had become members of the NCAA. In a move probably prompted by Walter Camp, the NCAA rules committee announced that the members of the old committee were invited to serve on the NCAA committee and that the old committee itself would be dissolved. The members of the old committee accepted the invitation, and from this point on the NCAA controlled all rule making for collegiate football. The organization ultimately devised a regional system of representation for its rules committee.

CHAPTER 12

MOVING TO THE MODERN GAME – RULES

1918 to present

Basic pattern set. The basic structure of American football had been fixed by the time of the first World War. In the period from 1918 to the present there were many, many rule changes, but no important new rules were enacted that significantly changed the way the game was played. There were, however, two very important changes that had an impact on the game overall. These were the two-platoon system and the provision for overtime in case of a tie.

Change bit by bit. It might be argued that a number of small changes over time can add up to something significant. Perhaps an example of this would be the use of hash-marks. Prior to 1933 a ball going out of bounds was put in play 15 yards from the sideline, but a ball that became dead (normally through a tackle) near the sideline would be put in play at the spot where it became dead. So, when a tackle was made two yards from the sideline, the ball was put in play there. In 1933 the rule changed so that the ball had to be moved 10 yards away from the sideline, and hash marks were added to the field to designate that distance. In 1938 this was changed to 15 yards, making it consistent with the out of bounds rule. In 1947 the distance was increased to 17 ½ yards (one third the width of the field), and finally in 1993 the hash marks were moved to 20 yards from the sidelines (the NFL moved them parallel with the goal posts). This, of course, greatly facilitated field goal kicking. In effect, the hash-marks performed the function of the old punt-out.

The ball. As mentioned above, the most significant change in the ball came in 1912 when the small circumference was reduced from 27 inches to 22 ½ – 23 inches, and the inflated pressure was set at 14-15 pounds per square inch (psi). But further changes were in order. In 1929 the circumference was reduced by one-half inch. In 1930 the pressure was reduced to 12 ½ – 13 ½ psi. This seems like a trivial change, but it was significant. It allowed the ball to be squeezed; it had some "give." This meant that players, especially passers, could easily grip the ball with the hand. It was the difference between gripping a wet bar of soap and a sponge. The circumference was again reduced by one-half inch in 1934, and in 1982 it was further reduced to 20 ¼ – 21 ¼ inches. Apparently all of these changes were made to enhance the passing game.

The extra point. Until 1922 the "try at goal" after touchdown required a drop-kick or a place-kick. In that year the rule was changed to permit a choice of kicking or scrimmage from the five yard line, and the term was changed to "try for point." If successful by either method, the score was one point. In 1924 the line was moved to the three yard line. In 1929 it was moved to the two yard line, and again in 1958 back to the three yard line, this time with two points given for scoring by run or pass.

Goal posts. For safety reasons the goal posts were finally moved to the back of the end zones in 1927, something that did not happen in the professional league until 1974. In an attempt to encourage field goals, the goal posts were widened from 18 feet, six inches, to 23 feet, 4 inches, in 1959. A change of heart came over the rule-makers in 1991 when the dimensions were changed back to 18 feet, 6 inches. This is the original Rugby Union size.

Substitution. The rules on substitution have gone from A to Z. In the rugby period substitutions were not allowed. Of course, the teams consisted of 15 men on a side. This non-substitution rule was made official for the American game in 1890. In 1897 one player could be substituted for another with the approval of his captain, but the departing player could not return. In 1910 a player withdrawn could reenter at the end of a subsequent quarter. This was changed in 1932 to allow any single substitution during a time-out or to replace an injured player.

With a shortage of players available in 1941 (presumably due to the draft and the anticipated war) teams were allowed to substitute any number of players, although they were required to remain in the game for at least one play. This provided the first opportunity for "platooning," or using different players on offense and defense. The NFL also allowed unlimited substitution in 1950. But, the college platooning system was abolished in 1953 when a rule was enacted that allowed a player to enter the game only once in each quarter. Then, in a turnabout, unlimited substitution, subject to time of entry restraints, was reinstituted in 1965. The two-platoon game did not change the way the game was played, but it did have an important overall impact. Twice as many players now played regularly, greater specialization was promoted, and the costs of fielding a team were substantially increased (scholarships, equipment, travel, etc.). Football became the only sport in which two sets of players, offense and defense, participated in the game.

Kicking and fair catch. The changes made in 1922 with respect to the extra point are discussed above. In 1923 the on-side kick from scrimmage was abolished. In 1926 a team incurring a safety was required to kick from its 20 yard line. In 1947 a place-kick or drop-kick for an extra point that fails to score a goal results in a dead ball. In 1950 the fair catch was eliminated, but it was reinstated in 1951; however, the option to make a free kick was eliminated. A punt that is not fielded becomes dead and possession is given to the receiving team in 1971. In 1972, 1973, and 1974 the fair catch signal is redefined along with accompanying penalties. In 1978 an unsuccessful field goal was required to be returned to the previous point of scrimmage. This was to discourage the use of field goals as punts. In 1986 the kickoff was moved to the 35 yard line.

Passing. The passing game was most advanced by the changes in ball size discussed above. However, other adjustments were made. By rule in 1920 an incomplete pass stops the clock. This of course provided a way of obtaining a mini-time out. In 1945 a forward pass was permitted to be thrown from anywhere behind the line of scrimmage (eliminating the old five yards back rule). The NFL had made this change in 1933. In 1982 pass interference could only be called if the ball was catchable. In that year it was made legal to intentionally ground (spike) the ball to conserve time. That rule was reversed in 1984 and then reversed again in 1990. The wording of the pass interference rule was changed several times as was the rule for roughing the passer. The penalties for these offenses also changed.

Miscellaneous rule changes. In 1927 a rule was passed requiring players involved in a shift to remain in place for one second before the ball was snapped. This finally put an end to the use of shifts as semi-momentum plays. In 1967 coaching from the sideline was expressly permitted. This ended a series of long and unsuccessful attempts to keep coaches out of the game. It was the last gasp of amateurism in college football. In 1988 the defense was allowed an opportunity to score two points if they should intercept a pass, block a kick, or recover a fumble when the opponents attempted an extra point. Although rare, this situation does occur from time to time. Finally, the rule-makers devised a way to eliminate the tie game, the first time since the short-lived 1881 rule dealing with the "block" game.

The NFL had adopted a provision to eliminate tie games as early as 1974. The professional rule provided for a modified sudden-death playoff in overtime. However, under this rule it was still possible for the game to end in a tie. The NCAA experimented with an overtime rule in its lower divisions, and then applied the rule to division one (big time) teams in 1996. To oversimplify a complicated rule, under this system each team is given a chance to score from the opponent's 25 yard line. If the score is still tied after both teams have had their opportunity, another overtime period is started.

CHAPTER 13

MOVING TO THE MODERN GAME – OFFENSE

1918 to present

Attributing new innovations. As we have seen, in the early period of football's development new innovations were copied by other teams in rapid fashion. Formations, plays, defensive schemes, and player techniques spread throughout the playing world. At that time it was fairly easy to attribute a new invention to a particular coach or team. As the game became more homogenized, however, it has become more difficult to give a particular coach or team credit for something new. This is also complicated by the fact that slight variations of new devices have been created, and then variations of those variations have followed. So, in the modern era we are often not able to trace accurately facets of play that are nevertheless important. Occasionally we can do that, and in the following, we will when we can.

The twenties. The decade between 1920 and 1930 saw further development of formations, plays, and techniques that had been initiated earlier. Two of the most successful coaches in the 1920s were Knute Rockne of Notre Dame and Robert C. Zuppke of Illinois. As might be expected, their success depended in part on having great players such as the four horsemen at Notre Dame and Red Grange at Illinois. Both of these coaches used as their primary offensive formation a modification of the single wing invented by Pop Warner in the pre-war years. But their teams also used the T formation, the punt formation, and the spread. The Notre Dame variation of the single wing was called the Notre Dame box. The emphasis was still on running plays with plenty of interference. Passing was used somewhat sparingly except when the opponents had a poor pass defense.

Rockne used a shift with great success as a semi-momentum play until the required "momentary" pause was changed to a one-second pause in 1927. Notre Dame's success, some have suggested, prompted the one-second rule.

Although huddles had been used in occasional indoor games played in earlier years (because of the noise), Zuppke introduced the regular use of the huddle in 1921. It caught on fast. There were at least three advantages to the huddle. Coming out of the huddle players could quickly assume a formation and run a play without the delay of complicated signals. The defense, of course, did not know what formation was going to be used, so quick-out-of-the-huddle had the same effect as a shift – producing defensive confusion.

Second, players could hear the signals better, and, third, the signals themselves could be simplified. This is because it was necessary to code the signals when they were given at the line of scrimmage so that the defense could not know what the play was going to be. For instance, a simple signal might be "four, three," meaning the number four back (perhaps fullback) will run through the number three hole (between right guard and tackle). If that signal is given at the line of scrimmage, it must be disguised, for example, as "six, right, four, zebra two three," the third and sixth numbers being the real signal. All such coding could be eliminated by using the huddle, and the only signal given at the line of scrimmage would be for the snap.

The Huddle

In his 1924 book, *Football: Technique and Tactics*, Zuppke distinguished between two types of running plays: the quick opening, and the wedge. The wedge, perhaps misnamed in view of earlier history, was simply the type of play that accumulated as many blockers as possible. The quick opening, however, had as its advantage that the runner hit the line very quickly. This meant that the defensive down linemen had to be held only briefly by a blocker and not moved out of the way. Also, linebackers and other linemen who would ordinarily assist would not have much time to get to the point of line penetration. This concept was more fully developed later by the Chicago Bears.

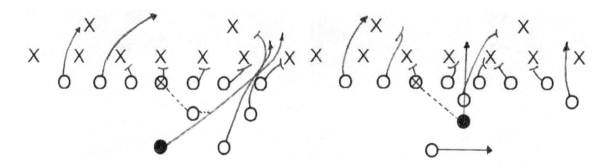

Notre Dame Box after shift from T formation. Left half carries off right tackle.

Zuppke's "quick opening" play from single wing.

1930 to World War II. With reduction of the pressure in the ball in 1930 and reduction in the size of the ball in 1929 and 1934, passing became easier and more frequent. The first of the all-time great passers was Sammy Baugh. He played for Texas Christian University for four years then joined the professional Washington Redskins where he played from 1937 to 1952. At TCU Baugh played tailback in the single wing. He was an outstanding runner, punter, and passer. This kind of triple-threat player was the key to winning for teams who played the single wing and punt formations which included most college and professional teams.

However, a change in offense was in the making in Chicago. George Halas, owner-coach of the NFL Chicago Bears, stepped down from his coaching position in 1930 and hired Ralph Jones as the new coach. Halas had played at Illinois under Zuppke, and Jones had been an assistant to Zuppke. Zuppke played the T formation as well as the single wing, and Halas had always been impressed with the T's possibilities. Jones was of like mind. Zuppke had advocated a modified snap to the quarterback as early as 1924. In his book he said, "If the quarterback is employed to feed the ball, he squats under the center, stretching his hands out toward the ball to force the center practically to hand instead of throwing the ball to him." "Practically" was the difference. In 1930 Jones improved upon this technique by putting the quarterback "under center." This meant that the quarterback put his hands up against the crotch of the center and received a direct snap into his hands -- nothing through the air. This was the first and possibly most important modification of the T.

Quarterback Under Center

The new method of delivery for the snap had four advantages over the old method. First, it reduced the frequency of fumbles on the snap. Second, the center would no longer have to look back between his legs, but could keep his head up and become a more effective blocker. Third, it put the quarterback closer to the line of scrimmage so that a run by him (quarterback sneak) would be more effective, or a handoff to a running back would be closer to the hole. Fourth, the quick handoff could be made either to the right or the left. This made possible the quick opener play on either side of the line. Zuppke had recognized the value of the quick opener, but by running it from the single wing, it was slower and could only be used on the strong side of the scrimmage line.

Jones corrected this problem and also began experimenting with the man in motion. A man in motion backwards or laterally had been authorized by the rules since 1910, and it had been used occasionally by other teams. Jones thought it had possibilities for further use with the new T formation. He also tried spacing the linemen farther apart to augment the offense. 1933 was the year that the professional league decided to depart from collegiate rules. One of the changes was to permit passing from anywhere in the backfield (previously only from five yards behind the line of scrimmage). This allowed the T formation quarterback under center to throw a very quick pass after the snap.

Even though Jones produced a championship team in 1932, Halas had to let him go and resume the Bears coaching job himself due to the Great Depression. There was no money for coaches. By 1937 Halas was able to hire Clark Shaughnessy, coach of the University of Chicago, as a consultant. Known as an innovator, Shaughnessy tweaked the T formation changes that Jones had introduced and produced a very effective offense. Shaughnessy spaced the linemen even further apart to magnify the effect of the quick opener.

He developed a set of plays which started with the quick opener dive over guard or tackle, then moved to a fake dive and give to the fullback running a slant on the same side. Then the series moved to a fake to the fullback and pitch to the other halfback for a run around end. Finally, a counter play was created in which the quarterback did a reverse spin and handed off to the fullback going to the opposite side. In all of these, line play was fairly simple, and interference was used minimally. Shaughnessy also introduced a number of new play-action passes. In the new T the quarterback was no longer a blocker or a runner; he was a ball handler and passer. The keys to success were speed and deception. All of these plays developed much faster than the single wing plays.

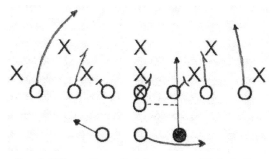
Bear's T formation. Quick opener. Right half dives straight ahead.

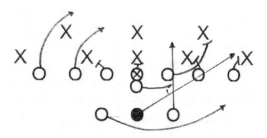
Bear's T formation. Fake quick opener, hand-off to fullback on slant.

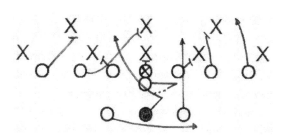
Bear's T formation. Counter. Fake quick opener, hand-off to fullback going opposite direction.

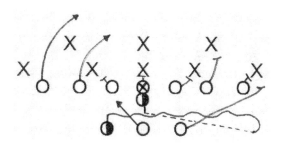
Bear's T formation. Short pass to man in motion.

As in life's other endeavors, nothing succeeds like success. The Bears ran all over everyone with the new T formation. In 1940 they defeated the Washington Redskins 73 – 0 in the NFL championship game, a record that still stands. Shaughnessy took his T knowledge to Stanford and turned around a team that had only won one game in 1940 to an undefeated team in 1941. Other coaches caught on fast. Frank Leahy at Notre Dame adopted the T in 1943 as did Dana X. Bible of the University of Texas. All of the professional teams had switched to the T by 1949 except the Pittsburgh Steelers who were still using the single wing. By the 1950s the vast majority of college teams were using the T.

Children of the T. If necessity is the mother of invention, then some innovative coaches found that variations of the T were necessary to produce their winning teams. The first step in a new direction was taken by Donald B. Faurot, coach of the University of Missouri. In 1941 Faurot was said to have invented the "split T" formation, meaning that the linemen in his offense were spread out more than in earlier T formations. This is highly suspect. Ralph Jones of the Bears had first spread the linemen, Clark Shaughnessy had spread those players even further, and Halas' teams continued the practice. At most, Faurot may have spread them a few inches more, or, it might be said that he was the first to do this in the college ranks. However, Faurot did introduce the option play from the T formation. It is not clear that this was in 1941 or a year or two later, but it was important.

The option. Although not the first option in offensive football (see diagram page 113), Faurot's scheme produced a technique that has lasted in one form or another down to the present time. He grasped the principle of the option from the basketball fast break. In that sport two men approaching the basket, one of them dribbling the ball, are confronted by a single defender. If the defender attacks the player with the ball, he passes to the other player who is free to make a lay-up. If the defender holds back and attempts to guard the other player, the player with the ball goes in and makes the lay-up.

Faurot applied this technique to the T formation at the end position. The quarterback, starting under center, ran to the right (or left) toward the defensive end. His halfback followed the same route about three yards to the rear. When the quarterback reached roughly the position of his tackle, the defensive end had to make a choice to attack him or follow the trailing halfback. If the latter, the quarterback turned up field and ran. If he was attacked, he lateraled to the halfback who went around end. With the option, the end does not have to be blocked.

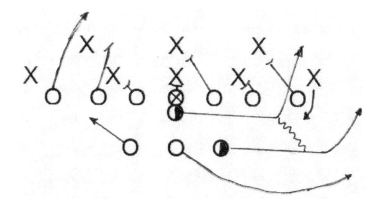

Simple option play from the spit T. QB runs to decision point and then opts to run up field or lateral to trailing halfback depending on what defensive end does.

The triple option. It is not clear exactly when the triple option came about. Faurot himself probably improved on his original scheme so as to offer the third option. Very likely other coaches experimented with this possibility. Bill Yeoman, coach of the University of Houston, is credited with inventing the variation known as the "veer" in 1964. Darrel Royal, coach of the University of Texas, along with his assistant Emory Bellard, is often credited with inventing the "wishbone" variant in 1968. The improvement over the simple option seems fairly obvious when viewed from hindsight. However, it does require a very talented and athletic quarterback. In this scheme a back (fullback in the wishbone, halfback in the veer) dives into the line between the inside defensive linemen. The quarterback may make a handoff to him if the defensive lineman (usually a tackle) on the outside decides to defend to the outside. This is the first option, and it depends on the quarterback's "read" of the defensive lineman. If the handoff does not take place, the quarterback continues down the line of scrimmage until he encounters the defensive end (or outside lineman) at which point the same election is made as in the simple option.

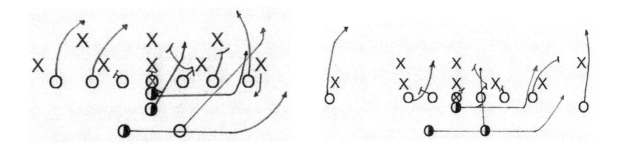

Wishbone offense. Fullback (behind QB) dives to right. QB fakes or hands off, if no hand-off, QB moves to end and confronts end where he either goes up field or laterals to trailing halfback

Veer offense. Right half dives straight ahead. QB hands off or fakes, if no hand-off, QB moves to confront end where he either runs up field or laterals to trailing halfback

What might be considered a fourth option developed quickly. When the end chooses to attack the trailing back, the quarterback may, instead of turning up field, execute a jump pass on the spot or take two steps backward and throw a short pass. Again, this requires a very talented quarterback.

The option plays turned out to be very popular and successful. Barry Switzer, coach of the University of Oklahoma, and University of Alabama coach Bear Bryant, picked up the wishbone shortly after Royal had brought it out, and they had outstanding success. Many college and high school teams in the 60s, 70s, and 80s adopted the veer or variations of it. Option football became the rival to the standard (old-new) T. In fact, coaches at the college level were experimenting with many different backfield formations and plays using the option.

Let's pass. Not all teams were playing option football, especially at the pro level. The original Chicago Bear's T was being modified and improved in other ways. Perhaps the greatest innovator of this period was coach Paul Brown of the Cleveland Browns (1946-1962) and the Cincinnati Bengals (1968-1975). His primary contributions were in the passing game. He originated the three-step drop back for the quarterback to pass. This was associated with a requirement that receivers run an exact-timed pass route so that the passer could throw to a point even though the receiver had not cut nor reached that point. In spite of the exactly timed route, Brown would also allow a receiver to cut in a different direction if he saw a defender in his path – now called "reading" the defensive back. This put great pressure on the quarterback to recognize the change in direction and quickly adapt to it. Brown had many assistant coaches, and a large number of them went on to become head coaches at the college or pro levels.

West Coast offense. One of those assistants working with Brown from 1968 to 1975 was Bill Walsh. After a year at Stanford, Walsh moved on to become head coach of the NFL's San Francisco 49ers. He brought Brown's techniques to his new team and added wrinkles of his own. His most influential contribution was to reverse the prevailing philosophy regarding the relationship between the pass and the run. The traditional view was to establish the running game first, thereby forcing the defensive players to bunch inward, and then the pass should be used when there was more room in the open field. Walsh reversed this. In his offense the pass came first, the run later. He depended on short passes using horizontal pass patterns that could dependably gain three to ten yards with a high completion rate. When the defenses loosened up to stop this passing attack, running plays could be used. This offense usually used a backfield with two halfbacks and the quarterback under center, but the formation could be varied. Walsh's system has often been imitated by other teams at the college and pro levels, but it requires a quarterback with very quick throwing ability.

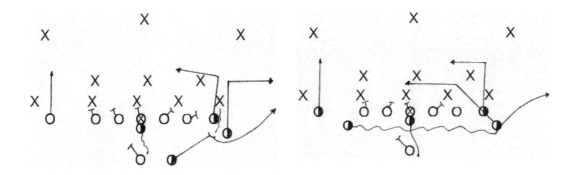

Short passing from the West Coast Offense. QB can pass to open receiver in flooded area.

Another West Coast pass with man-in-motion. QB again can quickly pass to open receiver.

Another west coast innovator was Don Coryell, coach of the San Diego State Aztecs, and NFL coach for both the St. Louis Cardinals and the San Diego Chargers. Coryell developed his new approach in the later days of his coaching at SDS (1961-1972). As with Walsh, passing became the primary offense for Coryell. But, in contrast with Walsh, Coryell emphasized vertical passing and deep routes. His offense favored the I formation and was especially known for a system of numbering receiver routes that was easy to learn and visualize. Coryell achieved considerable success when he moved with his new offense to the Cardinals in 1973 and later to the Chargers in 1978. As usual, other teams copied the offense.

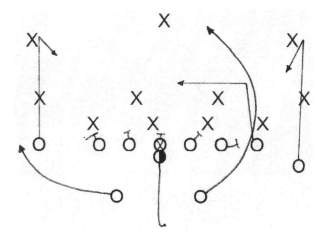

Coryell pass play with five receivers. Wide receivers do a comeback route.

Right half reads the safety and cuts accordingly.

Both the Walsh and Coryell systems have been called the "West Coast Offense."

The spread. As we have seen, the spread formation goes back to 1916 or earlier. All of the early famous coaches used it and diagrammed it in their books. However, it was not the main offensive formation. It was used to "loosen up" the defense when power plays and deception were not working. It was a particularly good formation for passing, but it could be used for running as well. As teams began to defend better against the new T formation in the 1960s, coaches began to turn to the spread as an alternative offense. A book written by TCU coach Dutch Meyer in 1957 called *Spread Formation Football* may also have influenced its development. The effectiveness of the spread was dependent upon a simple principle: spread the defense. By placing four, sometimes five, receivers wide, the offensive team could force the defense to spread out its defenders horizontally across the field. This could lead to all sorts of wonderful pass patterns, but it also removed defenders from the center of the scrimmage so that running plays could be successful.

Two types of spreads have come into use. In one the run is used about as much as the pass. This formation has two backs, the passer and the runner. The passer may line up under center with the runner about five yards deep, but more often the passer will take a position five yards deep, and the runner will be at his side. Either back may run directly forward or toward the end. On the usual passing play, the runner will block in pass protection. However, if the rush does not produce an immediate threat to the passer, the runner may run through the line and become a receiver for a short pass. In this system the option may also be used. The passer (now passer-runner) receives the snap and moves toward the line with his runner sidekick. He places the ball in the runner's gut and reads the defensive end (or tackle). If the defensive player moves to the inside, the passer pulls the ball out and runs to the outside. If the defensive player moves to the outside, the runner keeps the ball. Of course, many variations are possible.

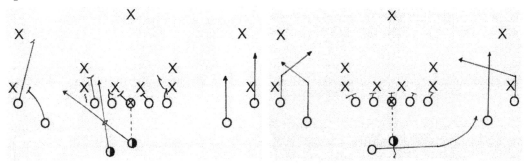

Option play from spread. Either back may carry.   Simple pass play from spread. Passer reads defense and passes to open receiver.

This type of spread requires a quarterback who can both run and pass well – a scrambler.

The other spread in use depends mainly on the pass. What type of pass play is used will depend on what the defense does and the quarterback's ability to read it. If the defense is playing zone (see below), the passer will call signals that put receivers in the seams of the zone or else flood a single zone with several receivers. If the defense is playing man-to-man, the quarterback will attempt to pair a speedy receiver against a slower-footed linebacker. Or, if there is a known weakness in the secondary, the offense can take advantage of a mismatch there between receiver and defender. The formation among linebackers and secondary will also dictate passing patterns. The offensive backfield will often consist of the quarterback alone under center or alone five yards deep. This allows for five receivers. However, if the defensive rush is strong, another back may be placed in the backfield for blocking. In this spread the quarterback must be good at long and short passes, but is usually not required to run. Signals are often called at the line of scrimmage because of the necessity to read changing defenses.

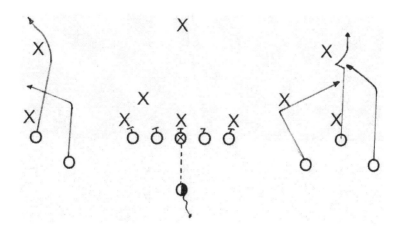

Spread pass play with five pass receivers and lone passer. Throw can be deep or in the flat, depending upon what defenders do.

Today's game a mixture. In both the pro and college game today we see a mixture of several offenses that have been devised over the years. In fact it may be difficult to identify precisely an offense or a formation as a spread, an option, or a T variation. One thing is fairly clear, however; today's pro teams do not want their multi-million dollar quarterbacks to get hurt, so they tend to play an offense in which the quarterback passes exclusively. When a run from the snapback is needed, a fullback or halfback is substituted for the quarterback, and the play is called a "wildcat." This is, of course, simply a modified single wing play. In college play quarterbacks are often scramblers who can both run and pass. This versatility can give more punch to the offense.

CHAPTER 14

MOVING TO THE MODERN GAME – DEFENSE

1918 to present

Reactive play. Unlike the offense, the defense usually cannot plan its play in advance of the snapback. It is always reacting to the offensive play. But the defense can plan and practice various ways of reacting to offensive maneuvers, and, unlike the offense, it is relatively unregulated in its formations and plays. So there is room for some creativity, and defensive coaches have been busy designing all sorts of schemes to stop the ball from advancing.

General strategies. The defense has one inherent advantage over the offense. It has 11 players who can pursue and tackle a runner, while the offense has only 10 blockers. On the other hand, the offense has its own inherent advantage. Only its players know where the ball is going and how. The latter advantage, however, is slightly minimized because the defense knows the down, time remaining, and yardage to go for a first down. So, thinking like an offensive quarterback, the defenders can anticipate with limited accuracy whether a line plunge, a long pass, or a field goal attempt is likely. The offense, on the other hand, has at its disposal deception and trick plays (fake punt, fake field goal, long pass on third and one) to counter the defense's anticipation. When the offense lines up with an unbalanced line or backfield, the defense shifts to rectify the blocker-tackler ratio.

Against running plays. The main defensive tactic against running plays is to put more men into the line of scrimmage and to space them tighter. The goal-line stand on the half yard line is the ultimate in this kind of defense. In the old days before the forward pass, teams used to line up eight, nine, or ten men on the line. That is occasionally still done today in the short yardage situation, but there have been changes. Instead of an eight man line, today's teams are more likely to line up with five or six defensive linemen and then have three or four linebackers charge the line at the snap. This has the advantage that the offensive linemen do not immediately know who to block, or they may miss a block on a charging linebacker. On the other hand, it does take a fraction of a second for that linebacker to hit the line.

In longer yardage situations a defensive team today is likely to line up in a five-four, a five-three, or a four-four defense if a run is anticipated. The possibility of a pass from anywhere on the field in today's game precludes loading up the line. The offense doesn't know whether or which of the linebackers will charge or stay back on pass defense. If a run is obviously in progress, the linebacker can move to the hole quickly and be almost as effective as a down lineman. These maneuvers are used when the quarterback is under center and there are one or more running backs behind him, that is, where a run seems likely.

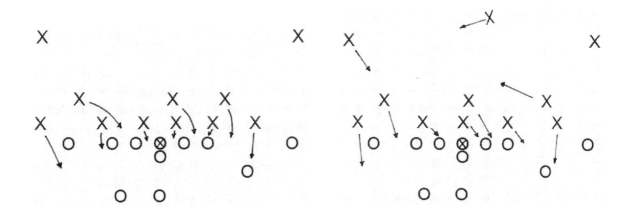

Very short yardage (goal line) defense. Linebackers crash. Nine rushers against seven blockers.

Defense anticipating run – longer yardage. Seven rushers against seven blockers.

Individual defensive play. Over the years defensive linemen have developed techniques that help them do their job. Of course, charging straight ahead is a fundamental beginning point. Today a lineman might also jump to the side as the offensive player charges forward and then pass by. He might also pull the opponent forward by grabbing his shoulders or arms and then pass by. If the opponent is relatively small, he can move under the blocker, lift him up and toss him aside. When charging low (submarine) he may not be able to tackle the ball carrier, but he can grab blockers' feet and legs and create a pile. He can also charge, not straight ahead, but in a slanting direction against a different opponent or into a gap. Or, he may step in one direction and then spin around and move in the other. All of these techniques make the blocker's job more difficult.

Cooperative defensive play. Most of the techniques listed above were developed in the early days, but more sophisticated devices have since been invented. These are sometimes called stunts. The simplest stunt is to have one lineman move to the right or left of his teammate and the teammate moves the other way when the ball is snapped. This delays the charge, but it also confuses the blockers. A similar stunt is to have a lineman charge to the right (or left), leaving a gap in the defensive line which is then filled by a charging linebacker. These maneuvers are often called "shooting the gap." An expansion of this idea is to have the entire line slant in one direction and then have the linebackers slant in the other direction. Of course, there are many variations of these techniques.

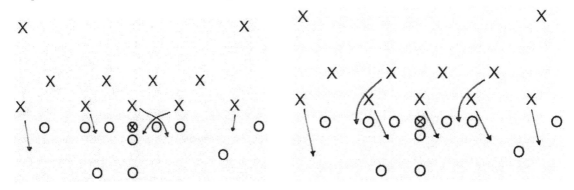

Simple charging switch.   Line slants left. Linebackers shoot the gap to right.

Pass defense. In defending against passes the defense is always confronted with a dilemma. Rushing the passer is very important. If the rushers can get to the passer quickly, he cannot get the pass off, or he is hampered in his throw so that the pass becomes incomplete. To make a pass rush more effective, more rushers are needed. On the other hand defensive backs are needed to cover receivers so that the pass can be batted down or intercepted. The more receivers who go downfield, the more pass defenders that are required. So, the defense must either sacrifice rushers for backfield defenders or sacrifice pass defenders for rushers.

Line play. The defensive line may line up in several ways when a pass is anticipated. A five-four, four-four, three-four or three-five combination of down linemen and linebackers are all used (sometimes called "the box"). The lineup selected does not necessarily dictate the number of actual rushers. A down lineman may drop back into pass coverage, or a linebacker may charge on the snap. The number of rushers will be determined in part by the offensive formation. If receivers are spread across the field, it will probably require spreading the defenders, especially if a man-to-man pass defense is used (see below). In charging the passer, linemen will know that a pass is imminent because the blockers will not charge forward; rather, they will gradually retreat, trying to keep the rushers from getting past.

Backfield play. The defensive backfield usually includes the linebackers, two players who play wide, called cornerbacks, and two deep players called safeties. Of course, there can be variations on this arrangement. There are two methods of covering receivers: man-to-man and zone. In the man-to-man play each defensive back follows a receiver and is responsible for defending against a pass to him. In zone play each defensive back covers a particular area on the field and is responsible for any pass that is thrown into that zone. These two systems go back at least to 1920. A variation on these systems is sometimes called "cover." This is a zone defense with either one or both safeties in cover mode, that is, they are not responsible for a zone, but rather back up the other defenders. Although not called "cover," Notre Dame coach Knute Rockne used this system in the 1920s.

The man-to-man coverage has two clear weaknesses: players can fail to pick up a receiver, and a receiver may be faster and able to outrun a defender. Likewise, the zone coverage also has two clear weaknesses: neither defender may be able to cover a pass thrown at the boundary between two zones (the seam), and a zone may be flooded with two or three receivers who cannot be covered by one defender.

The blitz. The blitz (earlier called the red dog) is a defensive maneuver in which additional rushers attack the passer in an attempt to disrupt the pass. The name comes from the German *Blitzkrieg* -- lightning war -- where forces are quickly concentrated to force a breakthrough. It is not clear when the word was first used in the football context, although it emerged into general usage in the 1970s. It is quite probable that the occasional use of a linebacker or two to rush the passer was tried in the early years. Since a pass defense in recent years will usually have only four or three down linemen, and the offense will usually have five blockers in the line, it becomes difficult for these defensive linemen alone to put pressure on the passer. The use of other players in "the box" to rush can bring about this pressure, but at the expense of sacrificing backfield pass defenders. It's the old defensive dilemma. Nevertheless, the blitz has become an effective defensive tool, and it is used by both collegiate and pro teams.

The secondary defense when a blitz is used can be man-to-man or zone. There will be fewer secondary defenders than usual because some will be participating in the blitz, so some immediate adjustments in coverage are necessary. The cornerbacks and safeties may have to move toward the line of scrimmage to fill the gaps left by charging linebackers. While zone coverage may not be especially effective in the non-blitzing situation, it becomes more effective with the blitz because the quarterback is forced to throw quickly and cannot wait for receivers to get far downfield. Invention of the zone blitz is usually attributed to coach Bill Arnsbarger of the NFL Miami Dolphins in 1971. At about that same time coaches began to bring one of the safeties in as a blitzer, and this technique became known as the safety blitz.

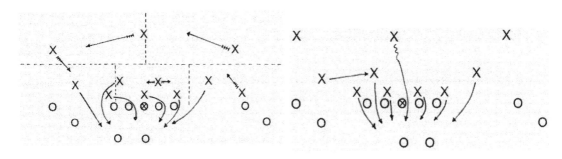

Zone blitz. Three down linemen and three linebackers blitz. Other secondary cover five zones as marked.

Safety blitz. Safety edges up toward line of scrimmage and charges on snap.

CHAPTER 15

EPILOGUE

What does our little history of x's and o's tell us? Does reviewing how football was played and the way that it has changed affect the way that we understand the game today? In my mind this history presents three themes worth noting. First, we can highlight the unsolved mysteries of this historical development. Second, we can recognize the process of organic growth that brought about the game. Third, the history shows that football has had a special appeal that has made it very popular. What is that appeal?

Mysteries. The first great mystery is why the ivy league teams abandoned the Association (soccer) game and adopted rugby in the 1870s. Several proposals have been advanced, none persuasive. First, Harvard led the move to rugby, and Harvard was a leading academic institution. Therefore, others followed. Arguably Harvard was not markedly more prestigious academically than Princeton or Yale, and, even if it was, the relationship between academics and football was extremely loose, as it is today. Second, the availability of *Tom Brown's School Days* caused a great nostalgia for the old scrummage. This is nonsense for two reasons: the book was a decade and a half old, having gone through numerous editions, and there could be no nostalgia for good old rugby because there was little conscious connection to rugby among the Americans. Finally, rugby is a more violent game than Association football, therefore the violence is what attracted our ivy leaguers. There may be some truth in this, but it seems a weak argument to explain the replacement the well-established Association game.

The second big mystery presented by our history is why there wasn't a simpler and earlier solution provided to the pointless scrummage? Alternatives are offered in our text, but other possibilities suggest themselves. One cannot help but wonder why the English didn't perceive the scrummage as pointless. It was a faulty solution to the problem of what to do after a ball carrier was tackled, something that could not happen in Association football. Camp recognized the problem, but his solution brought about further problems that had to be corrected (the block game, offside). Camp's solution, however, did lead, intentionally or otherwise, to further movement toward a more "scientific" game (his term).

A third mystery is why the rule-makers did not modify or abolish the offside rules when everyone was violating them. Or, for that matter, why didn't Camp and his colleagues foresee that the new scrimmage would violate the offside rules? There was a blind spot here. The players involved in a rugby scrummage were offside momentarily once the ball squirted out, but they did not try to block their opponents.

A fourth mystery is why football was not abolished in 1906. This question is purely political, and the answer lies in a careful analysis of the multiple political factors involved, something that has yet to be fully accomplished. John S. Watterson's book comes closest to explaining this mystery (see bibliography).

Organic growth. When we compare the Association game played in 1873 or even the rugby game played in 1876 with the present day game, we have no doubt that the modern game is not the same as the old. It is even difficult now to see any vestiges of rugby in modern football. Yet, at no time did anyone sit down and say, "Let's invent a new game, and we'll call it American football." Football was not invented. It was shaped, molded, and developed step by step. It evolved.

An analogy might be made to a group of children playing with Legos. Legos are little plastic building blocks that may be assembled in differing ways to make vehicles, statues, buildings, and other objects. Each child adds a Lego or two to the project. The project begins to take shape. What it will become may appear different to each of the children. More Legos are added, and pretty soon the project looks something like a house. Even more Legos are added, a correction made here, an improvement made there, and the structure seems to resemble a castle. What is significant here is that along the way when each child adds Legos, he or she is deliberately accomplishing some purpose, yet the end result is not the design of any one of them.

When we reflect on how human institutions come into existence, we realize that most of them are formed in this way. Where did the present day university come from? It started in the villas and castles of northern Italy in the twelfth century where learned men expounded on newly found texts from the ancient Greeks and Romans. There is practically no resemblance to our contemporary institution. The modern business corporation evolved from seventeenth century agreements between ship owners in England and Holland to pool resources and risks on long voyages. Step by step, one thing led to another. Such social constructs over the long haul are the product of purposeful human activity, but not of overall human design.

Football fits this pattern. The main characters in the drama are the players, coaches, and rule-makers. Each performing his own role, they have added something to the game as the years passed. They could have no idea of how the project would turn out. In fact, the project has not "turned out." It is still in the making, and new changes will follow in the future. At any given point in the development of football, say, when the downs rule was adopted in 1882 or the forward pass was authorized in 1906, it appeared at that time to most of those involved that the game had reached its final and perfect form. Yet there was an engine running that kept driving further change. That engine is still running. It is a perceived need for correction and improvement. This suggests that much of what we admire about developed social institutions is not due to any great creative insight of visionaries, but more to the natural tendency to bumble through by patching and mending.

The "scientific" game. A number of pundits, sports writers, and other observers of the American scene have suggested in recent years that football has replaced baseball as "America's game." Indeed, some would say that that happened a half century or so ago. There is no question that many sports fans, today and yesterday, have been fascinated by football and find it more interesting than other sports, although of course each sport has its legions of loyal fans. Is there something about this game that produces that fascination? Or is it a matter of promotion, hype, hoopla, and big bucks advertising? Certainly there is plenty of that, but I think there is something more, something about the game itself. What could this be?

A first thought might suggest that it is the violence and physical aggression that lends its appeal. Certainly the game still has that, although not nearly as much as in the early years. And it is true that displays of strength, tough tackling, fierce blocking, and sacking the quarterback somehow arouse our basic animal instincts. But boxing, hockey, and some forms of wrestling have the same appeal. None of those sports are in a class with football. Violence and aggressiveness may be factors in football's popularity, but hardly dominant ones.

Perhaps we should say that playing football is a comprehensive planned enterprise aimed at winning games. This is a unique feature. No other sport comes close to matching this. The play in football is all planned in advance with carefully thought-out formations and plays for both offense and defense. Players are trained to perform their skills, different for each position. Specialization, producing superior skills, is emphasized, and the use of two platoons and special teams is a natural outgrowth of this. Physical conditioning is essential. Practice as a team is essential. Communication in the form of signals is required to integrate the work of the various players on the field. Decision-making based on the other team's actions is also an important feature. Teamwork in the form of carrying out carefully timed tasks is at the heart of making the enterprise work. When mistakes are made or plans prove to be faulty, the old is rejected, and corrections are made both during a game and after, in preparation for the next game. Within human limits, nothing is left to chance. Football pits the capabilities of one team in all of these areas against the capabilities of the other. It is a game of brains, skill, planning, and cooperative teamwork.

To prove the point, we might consider how other sports measure up to football. Of course, individual sports like tennis, golf, or track and field do not involve teamwork or planning. Soccer, rugby, and hockey do involve teamwork, certainly to a lesser extent than football, but the factors of prior planning, precision-timed execution, and specialization are relatively minimal. Basketball and baseball seem to be the only rivals left. But here, too, we find that the factors of planning, precision teamwork, and correction are much less in evidence than they are in football.

We can suggest analogies that illustrate the appeal of football. The performance of an orchestra comes to mind. The composer plans, the conductor leads, the musicians, each a specialist, play together in carefully timed teamwork. Skill and practice go to make up a successful performance. What we appreciate is the overall result of this cooperative effort. The conduct of a business gives us another comparison. The production or sale of a product involves organization, planning, training, specialization of duties, correction of errors, and teamwork. We admire the business that beats its competitors through efficiency and good execution.

Finally, we should consider the analogy of military operations. This has been suggested many times over the history of football by players, coaches, and other observers of the game. Herbert Reed, a 1913 commentator on football, devoted an entire chapter of his book to the analogy. Charles D. Daly, West Point player, graduate, and coach, noted in 1921, "A remarkable similarity exists between war and football. This is particularly manifest in their organization. In both war and football we have the staff and the troops. In both we have the supply department, medical branch, and the instructional branch. In both, the importance of leadership is paramount." Note that Daly did not mention violence. Because war is violent and football is violent, it may be thought that the analogy relates primarily to the planned creation of violence. But the violent aspect of both of these activities actually hides the more important similarity. That lies in planning, training, cooperative execution of duties, and correction of mistakes.

Over the years this aspect of football as a planned cooperative enterprise has grown bit by bit, possibly beginning with Walter Camp's scrimmage rule. But it has grown mightily. Camp saw, perhaps imperfectly, the attraction of what he called a "scientific" game. That is the true appeal of football; it is the scientific game.

APPENDIX I

RULES

The Association Rules of 1863

The Rugby Union Rules of 1871

Important American Rule Changes

THE FOOTBALL ASSOCIATION

THE LAWS OF THE GAME

1863

1   The maximum length of the ground shall be 200 yards, the maximum breadth shall be 100 yards, the length and breadth shall be marked off with flags; and the goals shall be defined by upright posts, 8 yards apart, without any tape or bar across them.

2   A toss for goals shall take place, and the game shall be commenced by a place-kick from the center of the ground by the side losing the toss for goals; the other side shall not approach within 10 yards of the ball until it is kicked off.

3   After a goal is won, the losing side shall be entitled to kick off, and the two sides shall change goals after each goal is won.

4   A goal shall be won when the ball passes between the goal-posts or over the space between the goal-posts (at whatever height), , not being thrown, knocked on, or carried.

5   When the ball is in touch, the first player who touches it shall throw it from the point on the boundary line where it left the ground in a direction at right angles with the boundary line, and the ball shall not be in play until it shall have touched the ground.

6   When a player has kicked the ball, any one of the same side who is nearer to the opponent's goal-line is out of play, and may not touch the ball himself nor in any way whatever prevent any other player from doing so until he is in play; but no player is out of play when the ball is kicked off from behind the goal line.

7   In case the ball goes behind the goal line, if a player on the side to whom the goal belongs first touches the ball, one of his side shall be entitled to a free kick from the goal line at the point opposite the place where the ball shall be touched. If a player of the opposite side first touches the ball, one of his side shall be entitled to a free kick at the goal only from a point 15 yards outside the goal line, opposite the place where the ball is touched, the opposing side standing within their goal line until he has had his kick.

8   If a player makes a fair catch, he shall be entitled to a free kick, providing he claims it by making a mark with his heel at once; and in order to take such kick he may go back as far as he pleases, and no player on the opposite side shall advance beyond his mark until he has kicked.

9   No player shall run with the ball.

10   Neither tripping nor hacking shall be allowed, and no player shall use his hands to hold or push his adversary.

11 A player shall not be allowed to throw the ball or pass it to another with his hands.

12 No player shall be allowed to take the ball from the ground with his hands under any pretence whatever while it is in play.

13 No player shall wear projecting nails, iron plates, or gutta percha on the soles or heels of his boots.

THE LAWS OF THE GAME OF FOOTBALL

as played by

THE RUGBY FOOTBALL UNION

(1871)

1 A "drop kick" or "drop" is made by letting the ball fall from the hands and kicking it the "very instant" it rises.

2 A "place kick" or "place" is made by kicking the ball after it has been placed in a nick made in the ground for the purpose of keeping it at rest.

3 A "punt" is made by letting the ball fall from the hands and kicking it before it touches the ground.

4 Each goal shall be composed of two upright posts exceeding 11 feet in height from the ground and placed 18 feet 6 inches apart with a cross bar 10 feet from the ground.

5 A goal can only be obtained by kicking the ball from the field of play directly, without touching the dress or person of any player of either side, over the cross bar of the opponent's goal, whether it touch such cross bar or the posts or not; but if the ball goes directly over either of the goal posts, it is called a poster and is not a goal.

6 A goal may be obtained by any kind of kick except a punt.

7 A match shall be decided only by a majority of goals.

8 The ball is dead when it rests absolutely motionless on the ground.

9 A "touch down" is when a player putting his hand upon the ball on the ground in touch or in goal stops it so that it remains dead or fairly so.

10 A "tackle" is when the holder of the ball is held by one or more players of the opposite side.

11 A "scrummage" takes place when the holder of the ball, being in the field of play, puts it down on the ground in front of them, and all who have closed round on their respective sides endeavour to push their opponents back and by kicking the ball to drive it in the direction of the opposite goal line.

12 A player may take up the ball whenever it is rolling or bounding except in a scrummage.

13 It is not lawful to take up the ball when dead, except in order to bring it out after it has been touched down in touch or in goal, for any purpose whatsoever. Whenever the ball shall have been so unlawfully taken up, it shall at once be brought back to where it was taken up and there put down.

14 In a scrummage it is not lawful to touch the ball with the hand under any circumstance whatsoever.

15 It is lawful for any player who has the ball to run with it, and if he does so, it is called a "run." If a player runs with the ball until he gets behind his opponents goal line and there touches it down, it is called "a run in."

16 It is lawful to run in anywhere across the goal line.

17 The goal line is in goal, and the touch line is in touch.

18 In the event of any player holding or running with the ball being tackled and the ball being fairly held, he must at once cry <u>down</u> and there put it down.

19 A "maul in goal" is when the holder of the ball is tackled inside goal line, or being tackled immediately outside is caused or pushed across it, and he or the opposite side or both endeavor to touch the ball down.

20 In case of a maul in goal those players only who are touching the ball with their hands when it crosses the goal line may continue in the maul in goal, and when a player has released his hold of the ball after it is inside the goal

line, he may not again join in the maul, and if he attempts to do so may be dragged out by the opposite side.

21 "Touch in goal" (see plan) Immediately, the ball, whether in the hands of a player (except for the purpose of a punt out -- see Rule 29) or not, goes into touch in goal, it is at once dead and out of the game, and is brought out as provided by rules 41 and 42.

22 Every player is "on side" but is put "off side" if he enters a scrummage from his opponent's side or, being in a scrummage, gets in front of the ball, or when the ball has been kicked, touched, or is being run with by any of his own side behind him (i.e. between himself and his own goal line).

23 Every player when "off side" is out of the game and shall not touch the ball in any case whatever, either in or out of touch or goal, or in any way interrupt or obstruct any player until he is again "on side."

24 A player being "off side" is put "on side" when the ball has been run 5 yards with or kicked by or has touched the dress or person of any player of the opposite side or when one of his own side has run in front of him either with the ball or having kicked it when behind him.

25 When a player has the ball, none of his opponents who at the time are off side may commence or attempt to run, tackle, or otherwise interrupt such player until he has run 5 yards.

26 "Throwing back." It is lawful for any player who has the ball to throw it back towards his own goal or to pass it back to any player of his own side who is at the time behind him in accordance with the rules of on side.

27 "Knocking on," i.e. deliberately hitting the ball with the hand, and "Throwing forward," i.e. throwing the ball in the direction of the opponent's goal line, are not lawful.

28 A "Fair Catch" is a catch made directly from a kick or throw forward or a knock on by one of the opposite side, or from a punt out or a punt on (see Rules 29 and 30), provided the catcher makes a mark with his heel at the spot where he has made the catch and no other of his own side touch the ball.

29 The "Punt out" is a "punt" made after a touch down by a player from behind his opponent's goal line and from touch in goal if necessary toward his own side who must stand outside the goal line and endeavor to make a fair catch or to get the ball and "run in" or "drop kick" a goal (see Rules 49 and 51).

30 A "Punt on" is a punt made in a manner similar to a punt out and from touch if necessary, by a player who has made a fair catch from a punt out or another punt on.

31 "Touch," (see plan): If the ball goes into touch, the first player who touches it down must bring it to that spot where it crossed the touch line, or, if a player, when running with the ball, cross or put any part of either foot across the touch line, he must return with the ball to the spot where the line was crossed.

32 In either case he must then himself, or by one of his own side, either (1) bound it out in the field of play and then run with it , kick it, or throw it back to his own side or, (2) throw it out at right angles to the touch line, or (3) walk

out with it at right angles to the touch line any distance not less than 5 or more than 15 yards and there put it down, first declaring how far he intends to walk out.

33 If two or more players holding the ball are pushed into touch, the ball shall belong in touch to the player who first had hold of it when in the field of play and has not released his hold of it.

34 If the ball when thrown out of touch be not thrown out at right angles to the touch line, the captain of either side may at once claim to have it thrown out again.

35 A catch made when the ball is thrown out of touch is not a "fair catch."

36 "Kick off" is a place kick from the center of the field of play and cannot count as a goal. The opposite side must stand at least 10 yards in front of the ball until it has been kicked.

37 The ball shall be "kicked off" (1) at the commencement of the game, (2) after a goal has been obtained.

38 The sides shall change goals as often as and whenever (1) a goal is obtained, (2) it has been agreed by the captains before the commencement of the match.

39 The captains of the respective sides shall toss up before the commencement of the match. The winner of the toss shall have the option of the choice of goals or the kick off.

40 Whenever a goal shall have been obtained, the side which lost the goal shall then kick off.

41 "Kick out" is a drop kick by one of the players of the side which has had to touch the ball down in their own goal or into whose touch in goal the ball has gone (Rule 21) and is the mode of bringing the ball again into play and cannot count as a goal.

42 "Kick out" must be a drop kick and from not more than 25 yards outside the kicker's goal line. If the ball when kicked out pitch in touch, it must be taken back and kicked out again. The kicker's side must be behind the ball when kicked out.

43 A player who has made and claimed a fair catch shall thereupon either take a "drop kick," or a "punt," or place the ball for a place kick.

44 After a fair catch has been made, the opposite side may come up to the catcher's mark, and, except in cases under Rule 50, the ball shall be kicked from such mark or from a spot any distance in a direct line (not being in touch) behind it.

45 A player may touch the ball down in his own goal at any time.

46 A side having touched the ball down in their opponent's goal shall "try at goal" either by a place kick or punt out.

47 If a "try at goal" be made by a place kick, a player of the side who has touched the ball down shall bring it up to the goal line, subject to Rule 48, in a straight line from and opposite to the spot where the ball was touched down, then make a mark on the goal line, and then walk straight out with it at right angles to the goal line such distance as he thinks proper, and then place it for another of his side to kick. The kicker's side must be behind the ball when it is kicked, and the opposite side must remain behind their goal line until the ball has been placed on the ground (see Rules 57 and 58).

48 If the ball has been touched down behind the goal posts, it may be brought out in a straight line from either of such posts, but it may be brought out between them in which case the opponents may charge at once (see Rule 54).

49 If the "try at goal" be by "punt out" (see Rule 29), a player of the side which has touched the ball down shall bring it straight up to the goal line opposite to the spot where it was touched down and there make a mark on the goal line and then "punt out" from not nearer to the goal post than such mark, or from touch in goal if necessary, beyond which mark it is not lawful for the opposite side, who must keep behind their goal line, to pass until the ball has been kicked (see Rules 54 and 55).

50 If a fair catch is made from a "punt out" or a "punt on," the catcher may proceed as provided by Rule 44, or himself take a "punt on" in which case the mark made on making the fair catch shall be regarded (for the purpose of determining as well the position of the player who marked the "punt on" as of the other players of both sides) as the mark made on the goal line in the case of a "punt out."

51 A catch made in touch from a "punt out" or a "punt on" is not a fair catch. The ball must then be taken or thrown out of touch as provided by Rule 32,

but if the catch be made in touch in goal, the ball is at once dead and must be "kicked out" as provided in Rule 21.

52 When the ball has been touched down in the opponent's goal, none of the side in whose goal it has been so touched down shall touch it or in any way displace it or interfere with the players of the other side who may be taking it up or out.

53 The ball is dead whenever a goal has been obtained, but if a "try at goal" be not successful, the kick shall be considered as only an ordinary kick in the course of the game.

54 "Charging," i.e., rushing forward to kick the ball or tackle a player, is lawful for the opposite side in all cases of a place kick after a fair catch or upon a "try at goal" immediately the ball touches a player or the ground, and in cases of a drop kick or punt after a fair catch, as soon as the player having the ball commences to run or offers to kick the ball, has touched the ground, but he may always draw back, and, unless he has dropped the ball or actually touched it with his foot, they must again refer to his mark (see Rule 51). The opposite side in the case of a punt out or punt on, and the kicker's side in all cases, may not charge until the ball has been kicked.

55 If a player having the ball when about to "punt out" goes outside the goal line or when about to "punt on" advances nearer to his own goal line than his mark made on making the fair catch, or if after the ball has been touched down in the opponent's goal, or a fair catch has been made, more than one player of the side which has touched it down or made the fair catch, touch the ball before it is again kicked, the opposite side may charge at once.

56   In cases of a fair catch the opposite side may come up to and stand anywhere on or behind a line drawn through the mark made by the player who has made the catch and parallel to their own goal line; but in the case of a fair catch made from a "punt out" or "punt on," they may not advance further in the direction of the touch line nearest to such mark than a line drawn through such mark to their goal line and parallel to such touch line. In all cases (except a "punt out" or punt on") the kicker's side must be behind the ball when it is kicked, but may not charge until it has been kicked.

57   No hacking or hacking over or tripping up shall be allowed under any circumstances.

58   No one wearing projecting nails, iron plates, or gutta percha on any part of his boots or shoes shall be allowed to play in a match.

59   The captains of the respective sides shall be the sole arbiters of all disputes.

MOST IMPORTANT AMERICAN RULE CHANGES

These are the most important rule adoptions that created the game of American football. They are given in chronological order as new rules.

1876 Adoption of 1871 Rugby Union rules with slight modifications.

(Changed from Rugby Union rules) 7. A match shall be decided by a majority of touchdowns; a goal shall be equal to four touchdowns; but in case of a tie a goal kicked from a touchdown shall take precedence over four touchdowns. [Significance: touchdowns counted in scoring; in Rugby only goals (through the uprights) counted.]

1880 A scrimmage takes place when the holder of the ball, being in the field of play, puts it down on the ground in front of him and puts it in play while onside, first, by kicking the ball; second, by snapping it back with his foot. The man who first receives the ball from the snap-back shall be called the quarterback, and shall not then rush forward with the ball under penalty of foul. [Significance: rejection of scrummage; team can keep possession of the ball.]

The game shall be played by eleven men on each side. [Significance: previously 15 on a side.]

1882 If on three consecutive fairs and downs a team shall not have advanced the ball five yards or lost ten, they must give up the ball to the other side at the spot where the fourth down was made. Consecutive means without leaving the hands of the side holding it. [Significance: team cannot hold the ball indefinitely.]

1883 Point system for scoring: field goal 5, safety 1, touchdown 2, goal after touchdown 4. [Significance: replaced cumbersome and nearly unworkable scoring system.]

1888 The players in the rush line are prohibited from blocking with extended arms. [Significance: offside rule is disregarded and blocking by linemen permitted.]

Tackling is permitted between the waist and the knee. [Significance: strengthens defense, encourages more use of interferers.]

1889 The side which has the ball can interfere with the body only; the side which has not the ball can use hands and arms as heretofore. [Significance: disregard of offside rule is confirmed and interference (blocking in front of runner) is permitted.]

1896 Player cannot take more than one step towards opponent's goal before ball is snapped without coming to complete stop. [Significance: momentum plays, in theory, are prohibited.]

1904 Player first receiving the snap-back can run forward outside five yards from point of snap-back. [Significance: attempt to encourage sweeps and reverses and diminish mass plays.]

Six men required on line of scrimmage when ball is snapped. [Significance: extra players behind line of scrimmage reduced to diminish mass plays.]

1906 Time of game set at one hour. [Significance: attempt to reduce fatigue.]

Ten yards required to make first down in three tries. [Significance: attempt to encourage open game by making mass plays less effective.]

Neutral zone the length of the ball added. [Significance: prevents fouls at line of scrimmage and gives officials better opportunity to police.]

Forward pass permitted with limitations. [Significance: opens up game, reduces mass plays.]

1908 First pass interference rule limits defense and offense. [Significance: addresses a problem not anticipated when forward pass authorized.]

1910 Seven men required on line of scrimmage when ball is snapped. [Significance: eliminates another player in backfield and so reduces possibilities of mass plays.]

Pushing, pulling ball carrier prohibited; no interlocking hands and arms by interferers. [Significance: one of last vestiges of mass plays eliminated.]

Five yards from center limit on running forward and forward passing dropped. [Significance: opens up game.]

Game divided into four quarters of 15 minutes each. [Significance: fatigue reduced.]

One back allowed in motion laterally or backward before the snap. [Significance: offered flexibility in backfield formation, kept defense from setting.]

1912 Fourth down added to make 10 yards. [Significance: attempt to balance offense and defense.]

Field shortened to 100 yards; end zones created. [Significance: implements passing game, allows scoring by passing.]

Twenty yards beyond scrimmage limit on forward passes dropped. [Significance: opens up game.]

Kick-off moved to 40 yard line of kicking team. [Significance: adjustment required because of shortening of field.]

Pass caught in end zone made a touchdown. [Significance: opens up game.]

Size of ball changed significantly. [Significance: makes forward passing much easier.]

1916 Ball carrier's forward progress recognized as point of down. [Significance: reduces roughness and foul play in tackling.]

1922 Try for point after touchdown changed to allow kicking, running, or passing. [Significance: allows greater flexibility in making extra points.]

1927 Goal posts moved to back of end zone. [Significance: prevents injuries associated with running into goal posts.]

Players making shift must wait one second before ball is snapped. [Significance: eliminated the use of the shift as a momentum play.]

1929 Ball reduced in size. [Significance: made passing easier.]

1930 Inflation pressure in ball reduced. [Significance: ball could be gripped more easily, promoted passing.]

1932 Ball carrier down if body touches ground except for hands and feet. [Significance: prevents piling on and wrestling for ball on a tackle, reduces injuries.]

1934 Ball slimmed again. [Significance: made passing easier.]

1941 Modified unlimited substitution allowed. [Significance: allowed more players to participate, encouraged specialization.]

1953 Unlimited substitution abolished. [Significance: emphasized the "iron man" two-way player.]

1965 Modified unlimited substitution (platooning) reinstated. [Significance: allowed more players to participate, encouraged specialization.]

1967 Coaching from sideline permitted. [Significance: recognized the de facto functioning of coaches during the game.]

1982 Ball slimmed again. [Significance: made passing easier.]

1996 Overtime tie-breaker system authorized. [Significance: eliminated the tie, made play-off scheduling easier.]

APPENDIX II

ANNOTATED BIBLIOGRAPHY

There are many books on the history of football. Every university and college that has ever played big-time football has one or more histories written about it. So do the major conferences and leagues. Every coach that has achieved an outstanding record has at least one biography. All NFL teams have their written histories. The reader can locate all of these treasures on the internet. The bibliography that follows contains only those books, some of them obscure, that deal with the general history of the sport and give some account of how the game was played.

The asterisk (*) indicates the book is available free on the internet.

Alcock, Charles W., The Book of Rules of the Game of Football (1871)*

The rules of the Football Association and various clubs and schools in England with explanation. Outlines differences between Rugby and Association football.

Berry, Elmer, The Forward Pass in Football (1921)*

A booklet mainly describing the mechanics of throwing and catching the football. 25 pages.

Brooks, Philip L., Forward Pass: The Play that Saved Football (2007)

>*A history of the game centering around the adoption of the forward pass and its further development until the late 1920s. Much of the book is a biography of coach Jesse Harper.*

Camp, Walter, American Football (1891) (in The American Football Trilogy)

>*An explanation of the game as it stood in 1890 with discussion of the roles of the players at each position. Some history given.*

Camp, Walter, The Book of Football (1910)

>*An explanation of the game as it was played at that date. Contains informative diagrams of plays and offers a number of Camp's views and his philosophy of the game.*

Camp, Walter, and Deland, Lorin F., Football (1896) (in The American Football Trilogy)

>*An extensive explanation of the game as it was played at that time with illustrations.*

Daly, Charles D., American Football (1921)*

>*The famous Army coach gives tips on coaching, conditioning, practice, and offensive and defensive stunts. Plays are diagramed. He explains the connection between war and football and how similar rules apply. Blocking, tackling, and ball carrying techniques are discussed. Contains pictures of famous coaches and all-Americans.*

Danzig, Allison, The History of American Football (1956)

>*Contains much valuable historical data mostly in the form of excerpts of articles, correspondence, and interviews. Emphasizes careers of outstanding coaches and players.*

Davis, Parke H., Football: The American Intercollegiate Game (1911)*

> *The most important historical work for the period covered (1840s-1910). Gives a narrative history for 121 pages, then describes in detail many important games played in this period.*

Edwards, William H., Football Days (1916)*

> *A personal memoir of playing and watching football in the early days. Good descriptions of some famous games.*

Haughton, Percy D., Football and How to Watch It (1924)

> *The famous Harvard coach explains how the game is played. He uses photographs, mostly taken from Harvard games, to illustrate many of his points.*

Heisman, John W., Principles of Football (1922)

> *Coach Heisman takes his turn at explaining football, mainly for the benefit of younger players and high school coaches. He endorses many "maxims" to be followed ("always tackle low") and gives advice on training, drills, and attitude. Many play diagrams are included.*

Hill, Dean, Football through the Years (1940)

> *A history of football from its beginnings to 1940 in a little over 100 pages. Although the book contains a number of inaccuracies, it has many outstanding sketches and cartoons from the early era. It also has a section on pre and post game traditions followed by particular teams and their rivals and a description of various football awards.*

Ingrassia, Brian M., The Rise of the Gridiron University (2012)

This history deals with the relationship between big-time college football and the institution of the university. It demonstrates that the two entities are strange bedfellows, each serving the other, yet incompatible in many ways. The author seems to deplore this situation, but suggests no solution. The text repeats some of the history covered in the Oriard and Watterson books; however, the extensive footnotes and bibliography reveal thorough and original research.

Layden, Tim, Blood, Sweat, and Chalk: The Ultimate Football Playbook (2012)

A chronicle of football formations and strategies beginning with Pop Warner's single wing and ending with the no-huddle offense. Mostly deals with post 1950 professional teams.

Lost Century of Sports Collection, The American Football Trilogy (2012)

A republication of Camp's 1891 American Football, Stagg and Williams' 1893 American Football, and Camp and Deland's 1896 Football.

Lost Century of Sports Collection, The Lost Century of American Football (2011)

This is a republication of articles from newspapers and magazines of the nineteenth century dealing with football. It contains very valuable historical material in chronological order.

Lovett, John D., Old Boston Boys and the Games They Played (1906)*

A memoir about playing football under the Boston Rules by one who played under them.

Miller, John J., The Big Scrum: How Teddy Roosevelt Saved Football (2011)

A well-written book covering the crisis of football in 1905-06 and Teddy Roosevelt's role. The most comprehensive treatment of this subject.

NCAA, Annual Football Rules, various years, many available online

> *These annual publications contain the rules for the following season. They often contain much more information, especially about the play and results of the previous season. Many early editions edited by Walter Camp.*

Neft, David S., Cohen, Richard M., Korch, Rick, The Football Encyclopedia: The Complete History of Professional Football from 1892 to the Present (1994)

> *This book contains a massive amount of statistics relating to professional football. Each chronological section is preceded by a brief narrative account of the history of that period.*

Nelson, David M., The Anatomy of a Game: Football, the Rules, and the Men who made the Game (1994)

> *The most comprehensive treatment of American football history from the point of view of rules and rule-makers. Meticulously researched showing every rule change down to 1990 and every participant in the rule-making process. The reasons for the rule changes are explained as well as some of the politics involved. Nelson was an NCAA rule-maker for many years*

Oriard, Michael, Reading Football: How the Popular Press Created an American Spectacle (1998)

> *An interesting socio-philosophical study of football in its first few decades. The author is concerned about the <u>meanings</u> of football to its various constituencies (players, coaches, spectators, the press, readers of the press, faculties, etc.). Very well researched and thought out. The reader will not find much new about the game itself.*

Peterson, Robert, Pigskin: The Early Years of Pro Football (1997)

> *A well-researched history of professional football beginning with individuals who played for pay and clubs that started the pro game. Covers the origins of the NFL and major changes that have occurred in more recent years.*

Reed, Herbert, Football for Public and Player (1913)

> *A fairly comprehensive description of the game as it was in 1913. Contains some philosophically interesting comments about the game that had taken its last major steps to become American football.*

Rockne, Knute K., Coaching: The Way of the Winner (rev. ed. 1928)

> *The well-known Notre Dame coach explains his famous offenses and defenses in detail including the Notre Dame shift and the Notre Dame box that received great publicity in their time.*

Roper, William W., Winning Football (1920)*

> *The former Princeton coach discusses the training of players, tactics, and strategy with references to certain games and players of his era.*

Smith, Melvin I., Evolvements of Early American Football through the 1890-91 Season (2008)

> *The first 26 pages give a narrative history of the period involved. The remainder of the book reports games played between college, high school, and independent club teams for the time-frame covered. Very comprehensive and helpful to the historian.*

Smith, Ronald A., Big Time Football at Harvard, 1905 (1994)

> *This is the diary of coach William T. Reid of Harvard for the 1905 – 1906 football season. It is preceded and followed by a short biography of Reid before and after that momentous year. A fascinating account of the everyday tasks of a coach of that time. Unfortunately, Reid does not say very much about the meeting with President Roosevelt or the meetings of the rules committee.*

Smith, Ronald A., Sports and Freedom (1988)

> *This history, not limited to football, covers the early developments in college sports in the late nineteenth and early twentieth centuries. Smith explores the social values and institutions associated with sports and demonstrates that, in spite of the amateur myth, commercialism and professionalism have been with us from the beginning. He also explores the diffused or nonexistent control exercised over college athletics. Very scholarly.*

Stagg, Amos Alonzo and Stout, Wesley W., Touchdown! (1927)

> *The famous coach gives a brief history of football before his time and then gives further descriptions of the game from the time he played and coached it. Mainly a memoir, but it contains many details of historical interest.*

Stagg, Amos Alonzo, and Williams, Henry J., A Scientific and Practical Treatise on American Football for Schools and Colleges (1893) (in The American Football Trilogy)

> *An explanation of the game as it stood in 1893 by two of the most innovative and successful coaches of the time. Contains diagrams and explanations of many plays.*

Warner, Glenn S., A Course in Football for Players and Coaches (1912) *

> *This is an instructional guide with a great deal of "how to" information. It contains sketches and photographs illustrating many points. It also has numerous plays diagrammed in the T (or "regular") formation, the single wing, the punt formation and others.*

Warner, Glenn S., Football for Coaches and Players (1927)

> *This is an updated version of the 1912 book. It contains interesting comments on the forward pass and shift plays. More play diagrams.*

Watterson, John Sayle, College Football: History, Spectacle, Controversy (2000)

> *A very well written, well thought out book concentrating on what might be called the "dark" side of college football – injuries, professionalism, (play for pay), cheating, and dirty play. Attempts to regulate the game are carefully explained and reported.*

Weyand, Alexander, The Saga of American Football (1955)

> *A general history of American football with some diagrams of plays and formations. Emphasis is on big games and championships. Contains a list of all-Americans up to time of publication.*

Whalen, James, Ivy Leaguers Invent Football (1998)

> *This is a very good, if short, overall history of American football to 1925. It emphasizes the big games between ivy league contenders. All of the major developments in the early period are covered.*

Whittingham, Richard, Rites of Autumn: The Story of College Football (2001)

> *A very well illustrated history of football with emphasis on personalities (both players and coaches) and famous games. Accompanies an ESPN television series.*

Yost, Fielding H., Football for Player and Spectator (1905)*

> *The highly successful Michigan coach shares his wisdom in a format similar to that used by Camp and Stagg in their earlier books. Particular teams are discussed (the biggies of the time) as well as explanations of why football is popular and how it builds character. Excellent photos showing techniques of kicking, blocking, tackling, etc.*

Zuppke, Robert C., Football: Technique and Tactics (2d ed. 1924)

> *The famous Illini coach explains all of the techniques used by linemen and backs as well as his ideas on offensive and defensive play. Some of the ideas suggested are well ahead of the times (quarterback snap and quick-opening plays).*

INDEX

Akron, University of 66

Alabama, University of 130

American Intercollegiate Athletic Association – see IAA and NCAA

American Intercollegiate Football Association – see IFA

Army (United States Military Academy) 72, 103, 109, 110

Association Rules 4, 7

attendance 54

ball (American football) 106, 107, 116, 124

ball (Association) 8, 9

ball (rugby) 23, 24, 94, 95

Big Ten 73, 83, 87, 88, 104, 105

blitz 141, 142

block games 44, 45, 46

Boston Rules 16, 17, 18, 19

Brown, Paul 130, 131

California, University of 87

Cambridge University 2, 3, 4

Camp, Walter 36, 37, 40, 41, 46, 48, 57, 60, 64, 65, 70, 72, 74, 78, 79, 83, 86, 88, 90, 92, 100, 104, 111, 113, 144, 148

checkerboard 82

cheerleading 78

Chicago Bears 42, 123, 124, 125, 126, 127, 130

Chicago, University of 54, 65, 73, 87, 97, 104, 126

Cochems, Eddie 96, 109

Columbia University 5, 6, 19, 20, 22, 34, 40, 53, 85

Index

concessionary rules 21

Cornell University 72, 73

Coryell, Don 132, 133

DeLand, Lorin F. 57, 62

Denison College 109

Dexter Report 81, 85

double wing formation 112

downs rule 46, 47, 48

dribbling 10

Duke University 87

Eliot, Charles W. 69, 71, 81, 87

ends back formation 59

Eton School 2, 3, 9, 21, 40

Faurot, Don 128, 129

forward pass 91, 92, 93, 94, 95, 96, 97, 99, 104, 105, 106, 111, 118

Georgetown University 54, 72, 103

guards back formation 60, 74

Harvard flying wedge 62, 63, 71

Harvard University 6, 15, 16, 19, 20, 21, 22, 40, 53, 57, 70, 72, 73, 81, 85, 86, 88, 89, 90, 103, 104, 143

Halas, George 124, 126

Haughton, Percy 37

Heisman, John 37, 42, 56, 66, 92

huddle 122, 123

Hughes, Thomas 3

IAA 88, 89, 90, 104

Index

IFA 22, 34, 36, 39, 46, 48, 53, 54, 55, 56, 70, 72, 74

Illinois, University of 73, 77, 81, 97, 124

inch-kicking 39

injuries 66, 69, 77, 85, 86, 103, 104

Intercollegiate Athletic Association – see IAA

Intercollegiate Football Association – see IFA

Intercollegiate Rules Committee – see IRC

interference 38, 39, 57, 58

IRC 71, 72, 73, 77, 83, 89, 113

joint committee 90, 91

Jones, Ralph 42, 124, 125, 126

London Football Association 4

marching bands 101

mass plays 38, 39, 57, 58, 105

McCracken Committee 87, 88

McGill University 19, 20, 21

Michigan, University of 67, 73, 97

Minnesota shift 99, 100

Minnesota, University of 67, 78,

Missouri, University of 54, 128

momentum plays 57, 62

National Collegiate Athletic Association – see IAA and NCAA

National Football League – see NFL

NCAA v, 98, 100, 106, see also IAA

neutral zone 43

New York University 86, 87, 88

Index

NFL vi, 115, 117, 118, 124, 125, 127, 130, 131, 132, 142

Northwestern Tandem 79, 80

Northwestern University 73, 79, 87, 97

Notre Dame University 109, 110, 121, 122, 127, 141

Oberlin College 66

offside 10, 11, 12, 31, 39, 55

Oklahoma, University of 111, 130

Oneidas 16, 17

option plays 128, 129

Oxford University 2, 3, 4

penalties 53, 54, 92

Pennsylvania, University of 53, 60, 66, 70, 72, 73, 82, 85, 104

platoon football 117

Princeton University 5, 6, 19, 22, 34, 38, 40, 44, 45, 46 55 56, 61, 70 72, 73, 86, 88, 110, 143

Princeton V Trick 51, 52, 53, 55, 56, 71

protective equipment 26, 48, 49

pulling guard 58, 59

punt out 33, 34, 107, 108

punting 28

Purdue University 73, 97

quarterback under center – see under center

regular formation 43, 44, 100

Reid, William T. 89, 90

Rockne, Knute 121, 122, 141

Roosevelt, President Theodore 86, 89

Royal, Darrel 129, 130

Index

Rugby School 2, 3, 4, 5, 25

Rugby Union Rules 5, 19, 22, 25, 38, 87, 91

Rutgers University 5, 6, 19

scientific game 35, 36, 37, 146, 148

scoring 22, 23, 32, 34, 48

scrimmage 40, 41

scrummage 27, 28, 29, 30, 31, 32, 34, 37, 40, 41

Shaughnessy, Clark 126, 127

single wing formation 100, 101

snap-back 37, 41, 42, 43, 115, 116, 117

soccer 4 – see also Association Rules

spread formation 112, 133, 134, 135

Springfield YMCA School 65

St. Louis University 96

stadiums 81, 82, 110

Stagg, Amos Alonzo 37, 55, 56, 59, 60, 64, 65, 66, 83, 94, 97, 98, 111

Stanford University 87, 131

Stevens Tech 22

stunts 139, 140

Swarthmore College 85

T formation 100, 124, 125, 126, 127, 128 – see also regular formation

tackles back formation 60, 74

Texas, University of 127, 129

Texas Christian University 124, 133

Tie-breaker rule 118, 119

Tom Brown's School Days 3, 22, 143

Tufts College 21, 22

turtle back formation 60, 61

under center 124, 125, 126

uniforms 21, 26

Union College 86, 87

veer 129, 130

Villanova University 103

Virginia, University of 103

Walsh, Bill 131, 132, 133

Warner, Glenn S. "Pop" 66, 97, 98, 100, 111, 112, 122

Wesleyan University 53, 70, 85

west coast offense 131, 133

Williams, Henry L. 37, 59, 60, 66, 78, 89, 99

Wisconsin, University of 73, 87

wishbone 129, 130

Woodruff, George W. 60, 66

Yale University 6, 19, 21, 22, 34, 38, 40, 45, 46, 53, 58, 65, 70, 71, 72, 73, 78, 79, 85, 86, 88, 110, 143

Yeoman, Bill 129

Yost, Fielding H. 37, 64, 67, 97, 98

Zuppke, Robert C. 112, 121, 122, 123, 124, 125

Made in the USA
Middletown, DE
12 January 2020